Roses and Locoweed

Roses and Locoweed

✦

The Life of a Cowboy's Wife

Freia I. Hooper-Bradford

iUniverse, Inc.
New York Lincoln Shanghai

Roses and Locoweed
The Life of a Cowboy's Wife

iUniverse books may be ordered through booksellers or by contacting:

iUniverse
2021 Pine Lake Road, Suite 100
Lincoln, NE 68512
www.iuniverse.com
1-800-Authors (1-800-288-4677)

ISBN-13: 978-0-595-35933-2 (pbk)
ISBN-13: 978-0-595-80387-3 (ebk)
ISBN-10: 0-595-35933-7 (pbk)
ISBN-10: 0-595-80387-3 (ebk)

Printed in the United States of America

Contents

Foreword

This story is in honor of all the cowboy's wives who walked beside their cowboy on a path strewn with rocks, gopher holes, no money, worn saddles, moving to pastures always greener than the last and fields of locoweed. It's a story of fine horses, handsome cowboys, the seasons that bring a song to the heart or mud crusting the old worn boots, old West adventure and yes, the corny riding into the sunset and the perfume of roses.

This is also a story for the young things in Chicago, New York or any other city USA, who dream of marrying a cowboy. No, it is not meant as a warning. The readin' writin' and arithmetic of living as a cowboy's wife is the primer on how to live on love instead of money, how to be tough as nails, and how to appreciate a cowboy and his life that your mother never taught you.

By nature, this creature called a cowboy is a drifter. His love for being free and feel the wind in his face is no myth. He's got a have a good horse under him, and if it ain't a good horse, he's got to have the opportunity to make it a damn good horse. He's got to feel the woven threads of a rope between his fingers and the critter at the other end bawling the song of the prairie or mountain meadow. He's proud as a buck if he can feed his family from a freezer full of game that might or might not be legal, but he's also a stickler for the law of the land and honoring his word.

The cowboy's wife lives in his world of sweaty days, freezing your you know what off in January, welcoming a calf to this world as much as welcoming his own offspring, foregoing the red Camero for the dented pickup, and not figuring on retirement.

This story is seen through the eyes of the wife, the realistic one of the team. Forget about cowboys being realistic, they are romantics and all of them wish they'd been born a hundred years ago.

The young city girls who dream of loving a cowboy and the country gals who already know the score will chuckle and maybe wipe a tear with this account of the life of a cowboy's wife. Where did it all begin? As a horse-crazy teenager, the dream of riding horses led to the dream of marrying a cowboy. A fifty-six Chevy and a vagabond life, with no money in the jean-pockets, were the first years. There were also the rich times, not as in 'dough', but as in Wild West. The locoweed part of life were the lean times, the moving from ranch to ranch, the bad bosses, the leaky and sweltering houses and no end to an unsure, insecure life with the only guarantee that there would be more of the same. No, this story is not set in the 1800's, but life in the real west that still existed fifty years ago and today. Cut the Ford Ranger and the microwave out of the story and the life of a cowboy hasn't changed much from the old west. An impressionable young girl becoming a seasoned cowboy's wife is a tale of roses and locoweed.

1

From Dreams to the Real Stuff

None of the four riders talked as they rode into the hills. The silence of the dawn discouraged talking. Steam from the horse's nostrils escaped into the cool morning air. The grass, a shag carpet of fertile greens and in places high enough to reach the horse's belly, shed teardrops against the rider's boots. In the stillness, the saddle leather creaked, the only sound aside from the horse's hoofs on the soft earth and an occasional snort from a disgruntled horse. So far, they had located not one single cow or calf. Ragged patches of fog still clung near the river bottom and crept over grassy knolls, hiding the mammas and their babies. As the riders climbed higher, the heavy fog transformed into a curtain of gauze and at the very crest of the hill the riders emerged into a dawn washed sapphire blue.
"God, it's beautiful," he said, reining in his bay horse and turning around in the saddle to look at his wife.

I was a dreamer. Someday, I intended to make my dreams come true.

Throughout my adolescence, I wandered in a fantasy world embroidered with palominos, paints, black stallions and white Arabians. At age thirteen, I collected ceramic horse statues. I bought them at Woolworth because Woolworth sold the pretty figurines at a cheap price. There was never anything left in my mother's meager budget for useless nick knacks. I might as well have asked for a Rolls Royce than ask for a real horse. Instead, I devoured the pages of every horse book on library shelves and when I was supposed to read some dumb book assigned by my English Literature class, I pretended to misunderstand and checked out horsy books. The Black Stallion, My Friend Flicka, Thunderhead, and Will James.

Aside from reading, I enriched my dream world by writing horse stories and painting horses. On weekends, I glued myself to the television for every horsy program. Roy Rogers and Gene Autry were my heroes. Western and horsy shows were first priority on our snowy black and white television set. I preferred spending my money on felt cowboy hats and pearl-snap shirts. Spurs, bridles and saddles headed my wish list. Anything horsy beckoned me like a hummingbird drawn to the nectar of a red flower.

My mother just muttered, but then she muttered a lot. "Wieso brauchst du denn immer so was mit Pferden?" She asked in German because that is what she continued to speak at home after three years in the United States. She could not understand a daughter who wished for bridles instead of dresses and preferred Trigger as her hero.

"What do you want with that cowboy hat," she complained, "what is wrong with that pretty pink hat Tante Alice bought for you?" Some days my horse mania got to her and she scolded me about all the horse statues around the house that she dusted with the usual grumbling. I argued back, defiant and convinced I would become a great horsewoman.

"You just don't understand, I'm going to own horses someday."

She answered with her usual "Das ist doch Bloedsinn. What kind of nonsense are you talking about?"

My obsession made no sense to her. The family had moved from a tiny hamlet in the Bavarian Alps to the United States and had been left nearly penniless when my father died unexpectedly of a heart attack. My mother, in all of her German stubbornness, believed that horses belonged on the farm to pull plows and sleds. Riding horses belonged to rich landowners riding behind walled estates. Despite my mother's continuous head shaking in perplexed disapproval, my dreams persisted, but with her meager Social Security income, I accomplished no more than dreaming and scheming. With lights out and my bedroom door shut from my mother's world of reality, before sleep carried me to away from my daydreams, I invented brilliant schemes to become a horse owner.

Back to the reality of the living room: "Weisst du was das kostet?" She lectured in exasperation. "We are not rich, we can't afford such foolishness."

My mother, seeing no good coming from of this horse business, fretted weekly, but none of her fretting and muttering deterred my determination. I lived in a dream, and nobody was going to shake me out of that tree of fantasy. In my dream world, I rode a black steed, raced through meadows, waved to the crowd at rodeos and spent my life riding into the sunset forever. When hormones kicked in and boys tweaked my interest two years later, I added handsome cowboys to my dreams and the two of us rode into the sunset together. Forever. Of course, I did not advertise that part of the dream to my mother.

My closest contact with real horses after I arrived in the United States consisted of petting curious horses over barbwire fences along country roads. My mother made the mistake of allowing me to visit my girlfriend Lettie who had invited me to her father's farm near a nondescript town on the Colorado-New Mexico border. No one ever heard of Ignacio, but what did it matter? All I cared about was that it was a place for horses.

My fascination with horses expanded like a balloon in one instant, no more than two blinks of an eye on one lazy and warm morning. I climbed aboard a beautiful mare with a fiery copper coat. That had been my maiden ride. That summer day in hot and dry sagebrush country on the New Mexico border would change my life. The copper horse had been my introduction to the real world of horses, not just books, television, fantasies and horse statues from Woolworth.

On our first bright and hot vacation day, bridle in hand, we walked to the horse pasture past an irrigation ditch soothing the thirsty grass trying to eke out a living among the hardier sagebrush. The horses clustered at the far end, lazily swatting flies with their tails, and checked us out as if we were just another pesky fly, not interested in anything but dozing away the morning. They allowed us to bridle them without a fuss. Of course, my friend had to coach my bumbling attempts step by step. Then she helped me up on the mare's back. At that moment, my dreams solidified like a commandment set in cement. "You shall own horses."

My mother suspected that my dreams were more than passing fantasies after my introduction to the real horse world. She knew dreams are the seedpod that motivates a yet unborn reality. She surely had her own dreams, but she was afraid that at the naïve age of sixteen, I would venture outside my make belief world and buy a horse against her explicit orders.

She suspected I had been saving money from a part time job and stated in no uncertain terms, "Kein Pferd, verstehst du mich? You will not buy anything foolish like that."

"Yes, I know." I answered.

Confident that she had some control over her daughter, she planned a trip to Chicago to visit friends. I immediately collected my one hundred and ten dollars and promptly set out to buy a horse. I did not worry over dealing with my mother when she returned from Chicago. My exhilarated state of mind did not allow my mother to interfere with my dream-come-true.

Star was a little slip of a horse, a Pinto with gentle eyes and a compassionate disposition matching her eyes. She was a sweet and forgiving horse for a first time horse owner and tolerated my inexperience, forgave my blunders and behaved with the patience of a teacher. She tolerated my swollen sense of horse knowledge that in actuality fit into a buttonhole. I loved Star immediately. Nobody could have parted us, not even my mother.

The disaster happened two weeks before my defiant horse purchase. Another horse-crazy girlfriend and I rented a horse from our favorite stable. The stable owners figured we could ride when we foolishly represented ourselves as experienced riders, or perhaps they laughed behind our backs, but allowed us to ride on our own anyway. In hindsight, their decision turned into a major mistake. Feeling smug with a swaggering bravado, we requested to ride bareback because we decided that was the mark of a genuine horsewoman. Off we rode, deciding to race on this glorious day with nothing but sunshine and long stretches of open field. Our horses stretched out, annoyed by our unrelenting kicking, their hoofs pounding the hard ground along a lonely stretch of highway. I kicked my horse repeatedly until my horse had had enough. A heartbeat later I sailed through the air. My little horse was fed up, and unceremoniously, got rid of me.

One emergency room later, my shoulder wrapped and immobilized in a cast, my mother muttered with more conviction than ever. "Ach, jetzt siehst du was so schlimmes passiert mit Pferden." She was unfailingly convinced that nothing but bad happens with horses.

I figured the accident could turn out for the best. She had fretted about leaving me alone, vacillating between leaving and canceling the trip, but after the accident she felt secure in the knowledge that her impetuous and crazy daughter was grounded. She flew off to Chicago, knowing I could not ride horses for some time. She figured dead wrong.

I bought Star the moment my mother boarded a plane to Chicago. Now that I owned my dream horse, a broken shoulder could never to stop me from riding. Star patiently allowed me to climb on fences to get on her back. Of course, I had to ride bareback because I could not afford a saddle. My doctor and my mother's hair might have turned prematurely white had they known I rode bareback with a broken shoulder.

Star and I bonded in a day, but I suppose that I would have bonded with any creature as long as it had a mane and four legs. I buried my nose into her neck, the scent heady with sweetness and salt. I listened to her breath, gentle puffs as her black velvety nostrils widened and narrowed. Star welcomed my presence with a neigh when I approached her pasture. Soaring in heaven, I gave few thoughts to such trivial problems as expenses, how to pay for Star's pasture near our house, and even less thought to my mother returning from Chicago in a few days.

When my mother returned, she not only found out about my defiant horse purchase, but also that I had been riding with my broken shoulder. She raved; she berated me, ordered me to sell the horse, and muttered in between her fits. "Ach,

ach, oh my, now what?" She wailed and rolled her eyes heavenward, hoping for a solution from God who surely disapproved of this crazy scheme. For the next month, my mother barely spoke to me which had no effect on my perpetual state of ecstasy.

Her demands brought the same reaction as from a mule pulled against her will. I dug in my heels.

"Verkauf das Pferd. Immediately. You must sell it."

"No."

"We can't afford such nonsense."

"I'm paying for it, not you."

"What nonsense," she ended her arguments, punctuated with numerous German expletives.

The cold war between my mother and I silently continued for a two additional months. She hounded me with stories of doom and deadly accidents, pointing out my prior experience with my shoulder. Her nagging resulted only in digging my heels deeper and learning to perfect teenage deafness. I missed my father those times; he surely would have approved. He had been the adventurer, my staunch supporter and left a gaping hole in those struggling years of adolescence.

Every afternoon and weekend, I disappeared from home to trade the cold war environment for peace with my horse. I felt absolutely certain I knew more than my mother did although when she guessed my arrogance, she said with the manner of a German general," I lived longer than you and know better." Alas, she could not shake my belief that all old people, especially when they are over fifty, knew nothing about life.

Finally she gave in, or perhaps she gave up on her star-struck daughter who preferred to smell like horses instead of pink bubble bath. The day she conceded that her daughter would forever smell and think horses was marked by a remarkable gift. Despite her desperate finances, she bought a chinstrap for my cheap and patched bridle. She gave me the chinstrap as her peace offering and her acceptance of a future with horses, manure smells and visions of accidents. From then on, she helped me whenever she had a few pennies left over, knowing that nothing could take the horse out of my heart and soul.

I still did not own a saddle and did not believe it a problem. Despite my gross inexperience, my bareback riding skills improved enough to ride along side any Indian brave or cowboy on the range. So I thought. My mother never visited the pasture on the outskirts of Denver. It was just as well that she did not see her daughter ride Indian style or she might have been plagued with sleepless nights.

With typical egocentricity of a teenager, I thought of myself as the world's authority on horses.

Although I learned to ride within a few months, my training skills remained woefully deficient. Star was such a gentle soul and compliant Lady she cooperated with all my wishes and I developed an unrealistic sense of my knowledge and ability.

After the first year of horse ownership, despite my adoration of Star, she could no longer satisfy my desire for wild and daring excitement. In cowboy movies, horses always rear and buck and cowboys perform crazy stunts. I longed to ride a wild horse. With a wild horse, so I thought, I could show off just what a fine horsewoman I had become. I traded my tame and lovely Star for a sixteen hand tall black gelding with a hammerhead, Roman nose and bony back. The long black tail appeared to be his only positive attribute. Everybody considered him ugly. To me, he represented the embodiment of a dream stallion. Never mind he was a gelding that a stable wanted to get rid of because he was a spoiled and mean horse not suitable for dudes. The stable owner saw me coming from a mile away and had me figured for a good deal.

I fretted about how to convince the stable owner to trade horses. With my best horse—trading lingo learned from Western shows on television, I attempted to persuade the stable owner. Surely, I could make a deal he could not refuse. "I got a really good Pinto for you."

"Well, I ain't buyin' horses, don't need no more."

I played my trump. "How about trading?"

"What horse you wanna trade for?"

"That black one."

"We-ell, he's a pretty good horse, I don't know."

"I'll pay twenty dollars more."

"We-ell, let's have a look at your little horse."

I grew an inch just from ecstasy when the stable agreed to trade the big black horse for my little pinto. The stable, of course, ended up with the good deal. A year later I learned it should have been the other way around and they should have paid the extra twenty dollars.

I named my new black steed Stormy. Stormy did not take kindly to anyone doing anything with him, and without much ado, he let me know he hated everything except grain and carrots. Until Stormy, I did not know that certain horses have a mind of their own, and some horses cared less that I was a sweet, innocent horse-loving girl. I was stepped on, run over, bucked off, and kicked. My education about horses started with Stormy. After I limped home for the umpteenth time because Stormy bucked me off again and then had no guilt feelings about running over my prone body, my mother lent me the money to buy a saddle. She did not even mutter, throw a tantrum, or pinch her face with disapproval.

For fifty dollars, I found a used saddle at a riding stable. Later, I discovered the stable had nailed the saddle together in various places. Enter another stable spotting my innocence a mile away and figuring me for a good deal. My saddle was a prize example of the cheap of the cheapest saddles, but to me, the saddle symbolized a mark of stature, the mark of a cowgirl. Because we did not own a car, I rode the bus to the stable advertising the saddle. After the purchase, the saddle needed to get home. With the city bus my only option, I carried the saddle to the bus stop, dragging it on board. The fact that the bus passengers stared at the little teenage girl with the cheap felt cowboy hat dragging a saddle did not bother me in the least. My saddle represented my new status. A had become a real cowgirl. Let them stare, I thought. Let them be envious and admire someone who is a cowgirl. The thought that passengers believed different never occurred to me.

After my nailed together purchase, I had a horn to grab and the incidents of being bucked off and run over reduced dramatically.

I also learned to handle a spoiled horse through the Beery correspondence course, teaching the fine art of horsemanship and training by mail order. With money left over from feeding and shoeing my black steed, I sent away for the sorely needed home-study course. Bless the Beery school of horsemanship. They did not take advantage of my inexperience. The course provided everything it promised and then some. Beery figured that people who bought the course needed dead simple step by step instructions with dead simple drawings. They were right and for once, someone did not take advantage of my ignorance. I learned how to tie horses that pulled back and broke ropes and corral posts, another of Stormy's favorite activities. I learned how to teach Stormy to stand hobbled. At first, he fought like a rabid tiger, but Beery had his number. I taught my steed to follow without a lead rope. I even learned how to throw him if he made too much of a fuss. That last lesson probably convinced Stormy I was not a dumb human. Every page of the course brought small successes with Stormy's spoiled behavior. My ugly black horse changed into a docile well-mannered riding horse. At least he had turned into an ugly black well-mannered horse. I learned that my horse did not descend from a romantic wild horse breed, but belonged to a class of common horses that are spoiled rotten and no one had bothered to train. I felt immense pride in my success with Stormy but I also learned that I knew less about horses than I thought and that I had been operating under certain delusions about being a genuine cowgirl.

Stormy remained with me throughout high school until I entered college. Over the past year, I had learned to ignore remarks about his ugly head and body. Usually friends said nothing, but pursed lips, or a condescending nod of the head revealed their opinion. "So that's your horse? I see." Others commented, "Well, he's a big horse".

When I packed my saddle and boots to move into a dorm at Colorado State University, I learned how horses are supposed to look and my dreams diverted to a handsome horse without bony hips and a head reminiscent of a comic strip. At an auction the summer after my senior year in high school, I said good bye to Stormy. I sold him with good conscience as a well-trained docile horse. When the auctioneer sang out the final bid and added "sold to the young man with the black hat," pangs of sorrow crept into my heart. The time had come to move on. Stormy had taught me well. Soon I replaced my ugly black horse with a part quarter horse and part mustang and named him Laramie Streak after the country he had roamed as a colt.

I learned about Laramie Streak from a rancher's son more interested in dating me than selling a horse, or so I thought. His mother, who managed the ranch, seemed more interested in selling a horse than her son dating a horse-crazy girl.

By age sixteen, I blossomed into a teen with velvet skin, baby blue eyes and as trim a figure as a feline. With the speed of sound, I caught on to the benefits of being pretty. Young impressive boys were happy to buy presents, treat me to movies, dinners and dances, which led to calculations of how same boys could be of service concerning my horse. There were the boyfriends who shod my horse without cost. Another one hauled my horse from place to place just so he could be with me. It didn't take long to learn how to pick a boyfriend who could provide those expensive services I could not afford. At the prospect of a kiss, the various love-struck boys were more than happy to oblige.

George was my first real cowboy boyfriend with a real cowboy tan and bowed legs and best of all, he lived on a real ranch in Wyoming. George informed me he had talked his mother into selling the horse for a lower price. In hindsight, George's mother had been the one ending up with the good deal. She must have been happy that her little George knew a girl who would buy the horse she wanted to get rid of. George of course got something out of the horse deal. He spent time with the girl of his dreams.

We drove to George's ranch near Laramie where he attempted to impress me with the ranch but also sneak a little closer than I usually allowed. The Parker ranch dazzled and hugely impressed this wannabe cowgirl. George counted on my infatuation of anything western when he brought me to his prairie home. We caught Laramie on the windswept prairie as flat as a parking lot. Trees remained a word in the dictionary on the everlasting monotony of land. The wind whined over sparse dry grassland. A modest forlorn house, an uninteresting square encased in a white frame that had long ago succumbed to rough Wyoming storms, stubbornly squatted against the incessant winds. The weathered barn dwarfed the house and was in ill repair with part of the roof sagging under the unrelenting bluster of Wyoming elements. A rotting haystack towered as the only other obstruction in the monotonous flatness; its outer bales long ago turned moldy gray. Within my daydreams, the ranch exuded cowboy romance, where I conjured up images of mustangs roaming the prairie. George counted on this image.

George caught Laramie Streak, more than willing to trot up to his feed bag. He bridled him but did not use a saddle. He hopped on bareback and then helped me up behind him by lending me his foot as a stirrup. I sat behind George, a snug fit considering that the horse's rump sloped downward, toward George, exactly the way he had planned. Like that first moment when I spotted Laramie Streak on the horizon of the endless expanse of prairie, my heart again beat that familiar thump, thump. My head filled with fanciful notions of mustangs and riding wild horses.

After George introduced me to his mother, we sat in Mrs. Parker's kitchen and she convinced me that Laramie Streak descended from the Mustang, a genuine part of the Wild West.

"He's half genuine Mustang, yaw' know. There ain't many left."

"I can see," I said in my best cowgirl voice. "What is the other part?"

Oh, good ol' Quarter horse, you cain't get a better combination."

George agreed. "He's a beaut!"

"He sure is pretty," I agreed.

Mrs. Parker knew then and there that she had sold the old nag. Later, when I learned more about horses and actually got another notch smarter, I wasn't so sure if she had told the truth or simply turned a little girl's head with her impressive sales pitch.

Mustang or not, Laramie Streak belonged to the class of beautiful horses. His rich mahogany coat glistened under the Western sun, his head the right proportions with the look of intelligence in his liquid black eyes; his conformation pleasingly rounded, earning positive remarks at rodeos and horse shows. His flowing black mane and black hocks painted a splendid picture. Laramie Streak behaved like a gentleman, allowing me ride bareback at a walk, trot and lope. He listened, obeyed and showed an eagerness to learn.

I signed the deal in Mrs. Parker's kitchen and George seemed happy to deliver the horse to Denver, another excuse for a date. That summer before college, I pastured Laramie Streak in a nine-acre field on the outskirts of Denver, along with Cocomo, my girlfriend Judy's horse. When I started college, I hauled Laramie Streak to Ft. Collins where we won events in gymkhanas and horse shows. Because George was a Wyoming boy and not handy for a girlfriend who needed a useful and available boyfriend, I located a new boyfriend who owned a horse trailer and hauled my horse wherever my fancy struck. He hauled him here, there and finally back to college in the fall.

Although George faded into the background, he had introduced me to a new life of real ranches and real cowboys. Horses were still my number one dream, but cowboys were in the running for a close second place. My tempestuous adolescent heart thought it love whenever a handsome cowboy vied for my attention, although the real love remained my horse. I learned that dating cowboys meant taking part in the action I craved. I also didn't worry about smelling like a horse because all those cute cowboys also smelled like horses. The world of ranches, rodeos and western dancing became part of my life. Dates and boyfriends had to fit into my horse-routine and non-cowboys could not cut the mustard.

My mother started to worry all over when I decided that I needed to attend CSU because the university was seeded with cowboy students. "Ach, die vielen Kosten, wo finden mir das Geld?" Her pinched and worried look returned. She muttered a lot about college costs and horse costs, and where would we find the money?

I also fretted over college expenses and she said nothing when I sold Laramie Streak to pay my accumulating bills. I replaced my beautiful Laramie Streak with a cheap horse but at least the bills were paid off and the new horse cost only seventy-five dollars. Naturally, there was good reason this horse sold cheap. His crooked legs and his thin butt elicited derogatory remarks. Desperate, lonely and out of sorts because I didn't own a horse, I bought the sorrel at an auction with no guarantees and no returns. I nodded my head each time the auctioneer started his sing song bidding. "Who'll give me forty, forty it is, forty five, forty five, and now fifty, fifty, who'll give me sixty, sixty?" The auctioneer with the white cowboy hat turned up the bidding when I nodded my head again, swept away by the magic of the auction. Feet scraped on the wooden bleachers, horses snorted at the strange floodlights, and the auctioneer turned up the volume and speed. "This little lady says sixty, c'mon folks, this here horse is a gentle broke gelding, cain't buy better for one of yer kids, who'll give sixty five, sixty five, the gent in the back with the black hat, sixty five and now seventy, seventy, all right folks, seventy for the gent over there, seventy-five, seventy-five, seventy-five, going once, twice, seventy-five for the lady." I bought the horse with the crooked legs for seventy-five dollars. The auctioneer surely recognized a horse-sick girl and figured he had himself a live one.

When I turned twenty, my crooked and bony horse still with me, rancher Jim and rodeo cowboy Joe were in the running for the wedding ring. Rancher Jim cut a handsome cowboy figure, but ten years older, he seemed a bit too solid for a flighty young woman. Rancher Jim, the sole heir of a beautiful ranch where polled Herefords grazed lush pastures and horses roamed the hills beyond a sturdy barn shaded by ancient trees, wanted to stay home and raise kids.

Rodeo cowboy Joe could have been a double of the handsome Marlboro man. He roamed free and wild, following the wind to new adventures. He owned a '56 Chevy, a saddle, an anvil and his great grandma's rocking chair.

For the break between semesters, before the fateful meeting with rodeo cowboy Joe, I packed my bags and headed from Ft. Collins to work at the C Lazy U ranch in Granby. Rancher Jim sent me stamps as a hint to keep him in my heart, but I was swept away by a stormy romance with rodeo cowboy Joe.

On a mild midwinter day, fresh snow sparkling under a flawlessly azure sky, rodeo cowboy Joe and I saddled up to ride into the high country to search for elk. Above timberline, the horses broke through the snow's crystallized upper crust, sinking to their hocks. I reveled in the power of the Tennessee Walking horse Joe had chosen for our ride, most likely figuring that a good horse would earn him points. The intensity of a high altitude sun soothed the cold air and a pristine stillness was so complete that a hawk's screech shattered the silence as if shattering the sanctity of a church. The handsome cowboy riding next to my brown steed inspired wild romantic notions. His lean face, tanned the color of a redwood barn, framed by a black Tom Mix hat and a blue bandanna wound about his neck, was irresistible.

We spotted a herd of elk at twelve thousand feet, strutting across a field of snow, their heads flung high in arrogance as the masters of the mountain. I realized I lived smack in the middle of my dream. My heart soared as high as the hawk. Four months later, we were married.

2

Movin' Along

Denver is not a cowboy's haven. Not unless it's January and the National Western Stock Show. I figured that living in the city could not last forever. The cow town had long since disappeared. There are no dewy mornings to herd cattle on the range. There are no horses snorting with wild abandon on the range, no cows mewing for their calves. There are no wild cattle drives where you can shake out your rope in pursuit of a rangy maverick. There are no rides into the sunset with the last light illuminating the cattle range. There are exhaust fumes instead of sweet smelling clover. There are car horns instead of a whinny greeting the dawn. A steady hum of traffic, the growl of gears changing on buses and trucks replaces the pristine stillness disturbed only by screeching hawks and the craw-craw of crows circling high in the sky. There is black soot instead of billowing clouds of honest dust from a cattle drive. I longed to escape the noises and smells of a metropolis, but I longed to be a cowboy's wife more than I longed for peaceful pastures.

When rodeo cowboy Joe and I were first married, we lived in the big city of Denver by necessity because neither one of us were smart enough to figure out what to do now that we were a pair. Joe had to quit his wrangler job at the C Lazy U Ranch because they did not fancy married couples. I had no intentions of working at some non-horse related job and just tagged along wherever Joe found jobs. He found work shoeing other folks' spoiled horses, flighty racehorses, and a few that behaved without defiance and complaints. By the end of three months, Joe and I scratched together a steady income to put aside a nest egg after paying the rent on our furnished one bedroom apartment. We talked of little else but moving out of the noisy city. Joe's heart seemed as empty and lost as my own. We hated car horns, people in a hurry, and cement. Cement sidewalks, cement roads, cement buildings, and cement walls. The serenity deep in the Rockies had become a memory and an obsession.

When we moved to Denver, I left my basement bargain steed with a friend who owned a stable. We agreed that he would sell the horse for a commission and send me the rest of the money. He sold the horse but he kept the commission and the rest of the money. That was the end of my down payment for another horse. As a consolation, my new husband promised I would own many fine horses. Soon.

Our dreams were like a blown up balloon, rising with a lot of hot air inside. We figured that soon, the cowboy world would be ours for the asking. We were young and brazen with no doubts that Joe would find a job as foreman on a beautiful ranch someplace out West, and as soon as we were settled in the dream job, we planned to save for a ranch of our own. The first opportunity stared us straight in the face during Joe's budding horse shoeing career in Denver. Joe was tempted with lucrative contracts from some of the busier stables in Denver. My visions migrated from the small one bedroom apartment to a place of our own, a few acres with corrals and horses outside city noise and traffic. In my fantasy, I bought my own hotshot quarter horse. I missed Laramie Streak and the other bony horse I had to sell because Joe and I did not own a horse trailer. We did not own anything except our clothes and saddles, Joe's anvil and his grandmother's rocking chair. Joe's income didn't buy a bicycle much less a horse trailer, and we reckoned we better save for that move to our dream ranch. I accepted my fate that I married a cowboy and owned a cheap saddle with no horse to put it on. Regardless of a horse-less existence, my faith in my handsome rodeo cowboy never wavered. On warm summer evenings, when daydreams were brought to the dinner table, we conjured up our future.

"After I work for a few years, we can move back to where my folks used to own the old homestead and buy a few acres," Joe shared his dreams of spaghetti without meatballs.

I asked my new husband to describe where he used to live.

"It's real green and the Columbia River flows through pastures. There are islands in the river you can run cattle on." Joe painted a picture of tranquility and just the sort of place we might want to settle with a few good horses.

"And we could raise some Quarter horses," I added, envisioning shiny mahogany and palomino horses grazing lush pastures. "What about a place right here, we could move to Golden, or out by Morrison?"

"Naw, we gotta get out of here." Joe's boots were itching to move.

"But the shoeing contract is an opportunity, don't you think?"

"I promise, little bride, I'll get us that ranch. You wait and see."

My ex-bronc buster roaming the West from ranch to ranch, living in cow camps, and following the rodeo wherever the wind blew with enough good bull manure, spun new dreams. My own dreams of owning horses and riding into the sunset with a handsome cowboy would have to fit into the life of this restless cowboy. For now, the only riding into the sunset happened when we drove our '56 Chevy while the sun disappeared over the city of Denver.

Joe was my handsome cowboy, and I was an idealistic twenty and could wait for the rest of the dream. Naiveté was my guardian, time and youth my cheerleader.

When the opportunity knocked on our door to create a successful horse shoeing business, Joe's sensibility was out to lunch. His hankering for adventure bit him in the Levi clad butt and sent him pursuing a familiar life throughout his twenty-seven years. Instead of scratching the dirt to start a business, we packed our bags to answer an ad in the Western Livestock Journal.

Cowboy wanted near Yellowstone National Park for summer cattle work. That was all the enticement Joe needed. I too followed my yearning for romance and adventure, although my conscience continued to nag my common sense. My yearning for excitement of the unknown trampled the fleeting thoughts of security and opportunity to settle down. I ignored the voice trying to talk about good sense.

Joe had never known a sure thing, never knew security, drawn to the nomadic life as a rodeo cowboy. Since the last day of high school, he hankered to escape the hardships of eking out a living on the small Washington ranch where Joe's parents slaved from sunrise to sunset. I was addicted to the unknown adventures beckoning in unfamiliar hills and valleys and trusted that Joe knew his way around the cowboy world. The grass in Yellowstone seemed gloriously green. We chucked the Denver opportunity and moved to Targhee in Idaho. The one-building community outside of Yellowstone Park, complete with a leftover relic of a wind-up telephone, promised adventure. The promise did not include a lifetime opportunity, but a summer of riding and romance. We figured we could put off our quest for the lifetime dream job and a nest egg to buy our own ranch until the end of the summer. "After the summer," we both said, "we'll settle down on some wild and woolly cattle ranch. You'll be the foreman and I will train horses."

Targhee ranch turned out to be a gentleman's summer retreat, the sort where a rich man can write off enough dollars to cut down his income taxes. Mr. Finley owned several hundred cattle, roaming the outskirts of Yellowstone Park, sharing space with moose, bear, mountain lion and deer. He owned a few spoiled horses passed off as cow-horses for working cattle and riding miles of falling down fences that awaited Joe's fence splicing expertise.

Our homestead was one of those round one-bedroom trailers, the latest in traveling luxury. Thirty years ago, that is. The trailer had been parked under giant pines promising to become good conductors during frequent lightening strikes. The Targhee River, if overflowing, would move the trailer without having to be hauled by a vehicle. A private phone seemed an unavailable luxury in that part of the county. Neighbors used the wind-up telephone at the Targhee restaurant-bar-post.

You could get your mail, place a call and have a beer all at the same time. The boss owned a delightful cabin with a bathroom but also did not have a telephone; thus, we were not inclined to complain. For the boss it was a treat to get away from his business telephones in California. The boss said he couldn't wait to get away from his phones during the summer. At least he had a bathroom.

Unlike the boss however, we did not have a delightful bathroom in our trailer. We did have a leaning outhouse and soon learned the reason the outhouse squatted five hundred feet from the trailer. Strong outhouse smells were a fine attraction to the bear population that superseded human population. That posed a problem when we wanted to use the outhouse without furry company.

Aside from those minor inconveniences, electricity on poles and lines did not exist. However, the generator worked quite well, as long as I did not use the coffeepot and the lights at once. I quickly learned which combinations worked without blowing the generator: The hair dryer and two lights. The blender and one light. The curling iron and the crock-pot but no lights.

Despite a few inconveniences, this was home. Young love demanded no modern electricity, phones or in-home bathrooms. We lived under tall pines where the wind brushed and whispered through heavy branches and the Targee River rushed over boulders with a song of its own. Again, we experienced nature's symphony. The flutter of blue jay wings, the screeching of hawks, the rustle of a bush when a deer or elk brushed past.

Finally, I found my opportunity to ride. The black mare was a handsome part thoroughbred with an exquisite head and conformation. Pretty, however, turned out to be a spoiled horse; spoiled enough to be dangerous. If she felt like turning left when she was supposed to turn right, she reared in protest among other defiant maneuvers. The owner's wife admitted her fear and allowed Pretty to have her own way. Mrs. Finley gratefully allowed me to ride the mare. After several disagreements, Pretty and I came to terms with Mrs. Finley well out of sight. I used the skills I learned with my ugly black horse after the black mare decided to test my authority by flipping over on her back. Thereafter, Pretty behaved when I taught her to barrel race, explored Yellowstone Park or herd cattle. Mrs. Finley's fear, however, continued and she declined to ride Pretty after rehabilitation was successful.

Joe, on the other hand, had to do most of the work on foot. He fixed fence, and more fences. Two hundred head of cattle demanded little tending and Joe's complaints increased. Anyone who is a cowboy by now can guess about the complaints. "Goddamn fence," I heard every evening. His under-slung heels were not made for walking the fence line and his entertainment while fixing fence were bears that curiously sauntered past the cowboy cussing up a storm.

Bears were our constant entertainment and relief from boredom out in the boonies. They proliferated and outnumbered cattle. Most were the black bear variety and considered harmless. Close up in person they became a might imposing and they appeared at the most inopportune times. One fine morning the usual stillness competed with the distant rush of the Targhee River. I relaxed in a lawn chair outside our trailer, involved in the plot of a novel when something breathed behind my back. I heard the whoosh of a breath before I turned the next page. Ever so slow to cause as little excitement as possible for a bear standing on his hind legs, I backed myself into the safety of the trailer, shut the door, breathed and started my heart pumping once again. The bear stories didn't end with one incident.

The nightly bedtime ritual included walking to the outhouse. That walk was always a supportive affair. Joe carried the gun while he waited for me to finish in the outhouse. Daytime presented no problem for outhouse trips as bears waited for night to explore the attractive smells. During the daytime, I could scout the surrounding territory before entering the outhouse. At night, the black bear merged with the darkness among the trees.

Mr. Finley advocated for bear-democracy. One of our first conversations after arriving at the Targhee ranch was about bears. "We do have bears, you know."

"They any trouble?" Joe asked.

"No, they don't bother us. Just put the garbage away from the trailer." Mr. Finley attempted to convince us that the bears were no more annoying than horseflies.

Unconvinced, Joe asked, "They ever try to break into your cabin?"

"No, of course not, we secure the windows and doors. It's only careless people who have problems."

"Well, we haven't seen a bear yet." I added.

"You will, you will," Mr. Finley stated with pride and added, "don't run them off."

We quickly understood that Mr. and Mrs. Finley claimed this spot as their private wild paradise away from Los Angeles and he liked playing mountain man of the animal kingdom. He might have read about this romantic notion in novels. We tolerated more than one insult of bears because this was, after all, Mr. Finley's ranch.

One particular irksome bear insisted on sticking his nose through the tiny kitchen window in the trailer when I cooked the evening meal. The smell of bacon or hamburger lured the bear to the trailer and he or she couldn't resist the pungent odor of meat frying in a pan or perhaps he or she preferred cooked vegetables. Whatever the smell of the meal, Mr. or Mrs. Pest appeared. Joe insisted the bear had to be female. I figured only a male is this stubborn. I had no intention of finding out his preference. The visitor seemed a snoopy trooper, hardly frightened by my shouts, "Go on, get out of here." He always turned up at dinner or breakfast time to check out food opportunities. I learned to whack the pest on the nose with a wooden spoon. That worked for the moment. Mr. Bear shook the head and in disgust, lumbered off to find less annoying human habitats. One day the visitor must have decided that enough was enough. The smells were just too enticing to leave without one last try. He intended to invade the trailer to forage on all that bacon or heist a few apples. Joe happened to take his accustomed nap at noontime after a morning's worth of fencing when I spotted a huge hairy paw complete with menacing claws, trying to pry open the screen door. I tiptoed my way past the paw the size of a dinner plate to wake Joe along with his gun slumbering in the back bedroom. Joe alighted from the rear door of the trailer and deposited a load of buckshot in Mr. Bear's behind before he figured out how to rip the door off the hinges. Mr. Bear howled like a wild banshee chicken, galloping off into the forest, never to be seen again. We thought.

We duly related the incident to Mr. Finley, who fervently argued for the rights of the bears. After all, this was his little ol' wild kingdom and get-away place from human habitation and so what if a bear tried to share a meal with us in the trailer? We kept silent although our thoughts were far from agreeable and wondered if maybe the boss left his common sense under a freeway in California.

On a safe day, the boss and his wife away and us off on a weekend excursion to Jackson Hole, the pest broke into Mr. and Mrs. Finley's cabin just like a common criminal. Havoc and destruction followed. This boy showed no mercy toward Mr. Finley's kind heart. He tore a window off the frame, climbed in, cleaned out the pantry and had a party with canned goods, packaged food and plenty of cans of beer. The boss couldn't have been more livid. He did not want to believe that his bear would do this to him. Mr. Finley changed his mind about bear democracy and immediately instructed Joe, "Shoot the #*?%# if he comes back."

The bear must have known he pushed his luck. He carefully stayed out of sight and seemed smart enough to know when to quit and pick someone else as his victim.

Our summer ranch adventure ended when Joe refused to face another day of fence building. "That's peon work," he complained when he found another job on a ranch with greener grass. We moved to Pocatello. The green pastures were described as a Pony of the Americas ranch. We were immediately challenged with breaking the tiny horses in one month. Joe wanted to ride bad enough he ignored the size of the little horses and convinced himself they really were small horses and not ponies. I too wanted to ride and we decided here is our chance. We would live in a house with real electricity, a garden, and best of all, free beer.

The new boss, a beer distributor and an amateur horse breeder, said that his daughter could not wait to show several ponies. The rest he wanted to sell. "As soon as possible," said. Mr. Thompson and thought it worth good pay and free cases of beer.

The job seemed perfect, except for one hitch that Mr. Thompson explained only after we moved to his ranch. "I got fifty POA's," he warned us and waited for this to sink in.

"Me and my wife can handle fifty ponies." Joe assured Mr. Thompson.

"Well, you have to understand that all fifty ponies are not broke to ride."

"Okay, no problem" The old ex-bronc rider answered.

"But I need them broke to ride in a month!"

Joe thought a minute. Thirty days and fifty horses was a lot to ask, but not too much to turn down the job. "By golly, we'll do her." Joe convinced Mr. Thompson.

"So you can have them ready for the Golden Spike Livestock show and the State Fair?"

"You betcha."

We felt like we had just bitten off a hefty leg of a hundred-pound turkey and now had to eat the darn turkey leg in one sitting. Somehow, we would have to make it happen.

Mr. Thompson did mention the ponies were not broke to ride and forgot to mention the minute fact that none had ever seen a halter and spooked at the sight of humans.

Joe's years as a bronc buster in Canada were about to pay off. We couldn't afford the luxury of gentling ponies weighing up to six or seven hundred pounds by earning their trust before handling the little beasts. Besides, these were the rough and tough days when cowboys were expected to ride the buck out of the critter instead of communicating to them in horse language to avoid the inevitable rodeo.

Early the next day we started an emergency assembly line with time-efficient techniques and didn't worry what the boss thought of our fast-track breaking techniques since he lived in town. Joe roped the little horses; threw the resistant ones, followed by halters snugly fastened on their heads, tied to posts, fences and tires. Once the ponies accepted ropes all over their heads and bodies and tolerated being tied up to whatever was handy, two hot walkers and a couple of sturdy full size horses taught them to lead. Saddle lessons followed, with the rebellious ones learning to tolerate a saddle while they were left to buck until they decided it was a lot less work to tolerate the new contraption.

Sacking out followed with new temper tantrums in corrals and various places on the ranch.

At first, the ranch resembled an insane asylum for ponies. They bucked, ran, reared, kicked and snorted, shrieked, and whinnied for their buddies to come to their aid. The tractor pulled three or four ponies at once down the country lane to get them used to traffic and strange places. Hot walkers operated overtime until evening brought relief and the engines were allowed to cool off. The ponies walked and trotted up and down the lane, up and down. They moved in circles, around and around. The smell of sweat mixed with dust.

The mayhem finally ceased into an orderly adjustment. The last step consisted of getting on their backs. Since I never aspired to become a bronc rider, each pony experienced Joe as his first rider. After the crucial first ride, sometimes with less than effective bucking, I started to civilize the ponies for trail, pleasure and show riding.

The round corral saw plenty of action after breakfast to sundown. At the end of the month, every one of the ponies carried us beyond the safe confines of the corrals. The tiny horses, Joe and I accomplished our mission. Mr. Thompson expressed great gratitude. Pleased and impressed with his fifty gentle ponies, he never noticed the few little devils hidden in the furthest corral.

Ridden by the owner's daughter, one of my pet projects, a pretty snowflake POA, earned a first place at the Idaho State Fair in the Indian Costume class. Most of the other little horses sold at the Golden Spike Livestock show and auction. We were as pleased as the boss of our accomplishment and weren't about to have our arm twisted when the owner dropped by with several cases of beer from his wholesale warehouse. Neither did we mind the news that he expected us to buy a few more of the little horses. Apparently, Mr. Thompson turned a handsome profit buying green horses and selling them as a gentle child's pony.

Life after the big break-in slowed. Mundane and unwanted chores waited in the fields, the irrigation ditches, and the corrals. Along with breaking a new batch of little horses, Joe was busy with fence repair, cleaning corrals, and irrigating fields. After fifty horses, a dozen seemed hardly a challenge.

Soon Joe felt that familiar boredom, culminating in a distinct itch. He might not have caught the wandering fever had there been another fifty ponies to break. He started grumbling about the farm work. "Hell, I'm not here to irrigate the damned pasture. That's peon work."

I learned all too quickly that when a cowboy is relegated to fencing and farming, it isn't long before he slings his saddle into the back of the pickup or the trunk of his car and is on his way in search of greener fields and dustier corrals. Surely, the next ranch would be our dream ranch? At twenty-one, the handsome face of my cowboy husband still turned my head with romantic notions instead of practicality.

The greener grass in the new field grew in Woodland Park, Colorado where Joe worked previously on one of America's premier dude ranches.

Although the regular delivery of free beer tempted us to stay at Thompson's Pony Ranch, a cowboy cannot live by beer alone. He needs those strawberry roans that never been curried below the knees, a rope yanked tight around a steer's neck, or a good Quarter Horse to check on the herd in the south forty.

We moved. On move number two; packing of our worldly possessions became more of a problem than with the first move where everything fit into the trunk and back seat of our '56 Chevy. Joe's Chevy also balked at another long cross-country haul. We decided we could afford a new car because the job at Paradise Ranch had been secured. Being as impractical as two young kids, we tried to fit something fancy into Joe's meager salary and still manage payments.

We drooled over the Corvettes on the lot in downtown Pocatello, but couldn't figure out how we could fit great grandma's rocking chair, an anvil, two saddles and other personal accumulations into the two-seater or how that little sports car could pull a horse trailer. If we could ever afford a horse trailer! At the next car lot, we discovered a slightly used car that twinkled and sparkled in the reflection of our eyes. The turquoise Chrysler 300 convertible beckoned the cowboy and his wife. "It'll pull a U-Haul for the saddles, the anvil and the rocking chair with a few pieces of furniture," we reasoned.

After the hitch had been installed, a small U-Haul rented and the payment book in our pocket, we headed past the flat farmland of Idaho. Pocatello disappeared in the rear view mirror. With the top down, the world was ours as we cruised through Wyoming to our new home in Colorado. The engine hummed as steady as a sewing machine and not one cloud marred the azure sky as the song of the tires on the highway rolled away the miles.

Life was grand. Jump into a sporty convertible and take off to where ever we pleased.

Paradise Ranch, although a dude ranch, seemed just the sort of place to shower great happiness upon a cowboy. Summers were filled with rodeos. Four hundred horses needed riding, training, and re-training. Stagecoaches and wagons were polished and pulled by thundering six and eight-up teams hitched to the wagons with brass studded harness. The jingle of the harness, the thumping of huge draft horse hoofs created a splendid commotion. Daily rides with a hundred horses led into the majesty of the Rocky Mountains.

For the first time, I watched my cowboy husband ride a bronc during our weekly rodeos. The ol' thump-thump resulting from romantic notions returned. I too was hooked on the life of dust under a bronc's stomping legs, the whistle at the end of an eight-second ride, thundering hoofs of eight-up teams, and the clink-clink of harness. I reveled in hundreds of horses milling in a corral; chased out to pasture at the end of a hard day's riding. I had finally ridden through the gates of heaven.

We knew Paradise was our home forever. We were even meeting the car payments. However, 'forever' is a deceptive word for a cowboy. Four years is forever, especially for a cowboy with wild hairs to tame and itchy cowboy boots. Aside from Joe's itch to wander, trouble brewed at the home ranch. Joe, as the typical cowboy, figured he should be left alone by the boss, even if the boss paid his salary. Unreasonable demands from old Mr. Snell, by now a paranoid old geezer, finally nipped at Joe's headstrong cowboy independence.

In 1967, California beckoned as the place for genuine cowboys. California promised the greenest pastures of them all. By now, a simple move with our convertible was a joke. We accumulated household goodies and not curbing our appetite for ownership of furniture, stuff, horse equipment, more stuff, dogs, more stuff, and horses eliminated a simple move. We owned rooms and rooms of furniture, not to mention the saddles, Joe's anvil and grandmother's rocking chair. All those possessions could not possibly fit into a car. Then there were the horses. My Appaloosa, still a bit green behind the ears, had no traveling experience. "No problem," I said, "Wolf can learn to haul in a trailer in a day's notice."

Surely old Smokey could teach young Wolf to ride peacefully to California. We did not have the heart to leave old Smokey, a twenty-seven year old veteran, behind.

Suddenly, we had to figure out transportation for two big horses. The convertible was still our only set of wheels, by now immeasurably impractical for a drifter cowboy loaded down with non-drifter possessions. The convertible could pull a horse trailer which we still couldn't afford, but how to move the furniture, the two saddles, hay for the horses, the anvil, the rocking chair, a cedar chest, horse equipment, hats and boots? In addition to our worldly possessions, we acquired an extra passenger. Buddy worked at Paradise Ranch and he decided that California beckoned him as well. The lure of fresh green pastures, especially on a big cattle ranch, was enough to cause itchy feet for Buddy with no amount of foot powder eliminating the itch.

Buddy, unfortunately, although expected, was flat broke and unable to contribute a vehicle. He blew up his fifty-eight Cadillac when he tried to outrun the cops in a high-speed chase after he left a cowboy drinking party. He just left the Cadillac behind trees where he had driven out of sight from the law. With Buddy's Caddy out of commission and too expensive to repair, we were left with seeking other possibilities. Most were too expensive or just not adequate. Finally, searching the country for something cheap, road-worthy and able to haul horses, hay, the anvil and saddles, Buddy and Joe stumbled upon their eastern star shining brightly at a car lot where 'Mighty Sam's Best Car Deals' promised to beat any dealer in the entire county. Joe and Buddy realized that the advertisement might have been an over-statement, but the dollar sign caught their eye.

We were now proud owners of a 1949 Studebaker pickup. For its age, the pickup appeared to be in fine shape. Buddy and Joe bragged that the engine would run all the way to California and the tires still had some tread left. Building a stock rack for our two horses became the next hurdle.

Buddy and Joe said they could easily build a real fancy and sturdy stock rack in a few days before they disappeared in the lumbar yard. "Them's gonna be the best-ever-stock-rack, mark my word," Buddy grinned.

They hammered, sawed, measured, nailed and cussed, the back yard smelled like sawdust, but the stock rack did take shape. It towered over the fragile little pickup, growing higher every day. They finally assembled the best-ever-stock-rack, built from sturdy two by six pine planks, with a fancy feed bunk perched high above the cab and extending over the cab to hold the hay and anvil. Buddy and Joe thought of everything. The gate swung down to the ground to provide a ramp, never mind that it seemed too steep for a horse to climb. The best-ever-stock-rack-builders assured my skeptical mind that our horses would learn to get a running start and leap right on up into the bed of the pickup.

"Okay-dokay" I said.

The heavy gate needed two strong bodies to lift up or down with extra care that it wouldn't fall and crush anyone in the way. I did not reserve my doubts when I surveyed the 'best-ever-stock-racks. They seemed suited for a semi truck and I voiced my worries. "They're so BIG, they look so HEAVY!"

Buddy and Joe assured me this was no problem. "Naw, they'll do real good."

"You sure that ol' Studebaker can handle this? Won't it be top heavy?"

"Naw," Buddy assured me again, "This ol' girl is gonna do just fine." He petted the pickup.

I figured Buddy as a dreamer. "What about the horses? It's so high up from the ground to the pickup bed?"

Buddy, real proud of their project and confident as a hound dog with a fresh scent, explained to this skeptic the finer points of the stock racks and the best-ever-tail-ramp. "No problem, see, we built the best ramp out of the tailgate, they'll walk right up."

"Okay-dokey," I said again and kept further thoughts to myself.

The best-ever-stock-rack did have everything a horse could wish for. High handcrafted pine—board sides. Hay to munch on the best-ever-over-the-cab feed-rack, rubber mats and a 200-pound ramp locked securely behind the horse's tails. The problem was that the horses did not care for all those fancy extras. The boys and I spent the next day trying to convince Wolf and Smokey they liked riding in the pickup. After so many daylight hours, we finally convinced the two horses how lucky they were to have such a fine conveyance. They played along by learning to take a running leap into the pickup primarily because that was the only place they could find their portion of grain. Each time they jumped into the pickup, the old Studebaker rocked and protested with squeaks and groans.

Loading the pickup with the painstaking care of a load-master followed the horse loading lessons. On top of the feed bunk, Joe stored his anvil and a couple of bales of hay. He slid the ribbed rubber mats on the floor of the bed. Nothing added or deposited into the pickup seemed to weigh less than two hundred pounds. We also crammed and loaded the U-Haul to the roof and were lucky that the Chrysler convertible sported a strong V-8. Buddy and Joe elected to share driving the Studebaker. With all that weight on the bed, they thought that two strong cowboys should manage the pickup. I would follow in luxury.

Out of Colorado Springs, so far so good. The Studebaker chugged along without protest. The horses behaved as well as could be expected. Wolf Creek pass was the first obstacle to conquer. Buddy and Joe showed good faith in the Stude-baker and the old crate did not disappoint them. In lowest gear, it rounded curves and valiantly climbed the steep pass. We approached the top of the pass, looking forward to descending to Pagosa Springs when all hell broke loose. Wolf decided he was bored. The defiant youngster climbed the best-ever-stock-racks although he failed to climb out of his confinement. In one way that was good, in another way it was not so good. After several attempts, Wolf lost his footing and flipped upside down. A tremendous thump and the pickup rocking from side to left a clue for Joe and Buddy that all was not well.

We parked our vehicles along side the road at the top of Wolf Creek pass. Joe and Buddy lowered the two 200-pound ramp to investigate the commotion.

"Oh shit," we said at the first sight of Wolf upside down with Smokey stand-ing over Wolf. We decided that the first order of the process had to be pulling Smokey out backward. Smokey did not want to step on Wolf and balked. He intended to move not even one inch. Eventually after much sweet-talking and a variety of curses, we extracted Smokey a few inches at a time. Wolf remained upside down. Now that Wolf didn't have Smokey straddling his body, he strug-gled, kicked and broke those side rails that he hadn't already splintered during his climbing attempts. It appeared he had no intention of standing on his four legs. We pulled on the halter rope, cajoled, nudged; tempted him with grain, cursed, but failed to budge Wolf off his back.

In the meantime, the scene attracted attention. Folks drove by mighty slow to take in the entire spectacle, which appeared to be out of a 'Beverly Hillbilly' show. Some folks grabbed their cameras. We ignored the spectators and stopped all attempts for a conference and brain storming session.

"I had enough of that little shit." Joe stated. "By god, he'll either drown or get up!"

"Just shoot him!" I didn't really mean the shooting part.

Buddy chimed in. "Hell, he's gonna find out standin' is better than dyin'."

On our last chance attempt, Buddy pulled on the halter rope while Joe trick-led water into Wolf's nostrils.

"I don't care if he drowns." I announced without conviction.

With a giant heave, Wolf staggered to an upright position. Perhaps he under-stood our threats or felt terrified by water in his nostrils. During his attempt to get up, a sickening splintering of wood caught our attention. Wolf had kicked out additional best-ever-stock rack-boards.

The next problem occurred. The horses could not be hauled with broken side rails. Somehow, the best-ever-stock-racks had to be repaired before driving down the pass to Pagosa Springs. Buddy and Joe found a fine solution by cutting young aspen poles to replace the boards, and since no nails were available, a piece of leather cut into thongs turned into a fine solution to hold the poles in place. The best-ever-stock-racks started to take on a certain character.

We reloaded the horses and crossed our fingers that Wolf learned his lesson. He avoided his climbing exercises, but we were nervous about a repetition of events. Down the pass we drove, in low gear to keep the brakes from smoking. In Pagosa Springs, we headed straight to the nearest lumbar yard to buy a large side of solid plywood. At the yard, Joe and Buddy nailed the smooth plywood to the inside of the right side of the best-ever-stock-rack.

"Ok, that's gonna do it." Buddy thumped the patched best-ever-stock-racks. They were as good as new. They weighed an additional one hundred pounds.

The next hitch occurred the following day, after an early stop along the Colorado River. September in the Mojave Desert is no place for humans or horses. We headed into a hellish oven with the thermostat cranked to 120 degrees. The smell of sweat mixed with exhaust fumes and the desert sun sapped the life out of everything from tarantulas to humans. We felt real sorry for ourselves before we remembered to worry more about the horses baking under a blast furnace. I invented shade for the poor creatures by stretching a white bed sheet over the horses and tying it to the best-ever-stock-racks. This worked well along with frequent stops for water.

The horses survived, although my dignity did not. Every day the Studebaker changed more and more into the old rattletrap out of the Rounders or Beverly Hillbillies. Tourists snapped away with their Kodaks as I drove a respectable distance behind the pickup to make sure I was not associated with 'that bunch'.

Outside the city limits of Mojave, we headed for the Colorado River where we discovered a sandy, willow enclosed camping spot to unload the horses. Buddy jumped bareback on Smokey's back while I jumped on Wolf and we headed for the river where we splashed and played for a while, soaking up the cool water. Both horses instinctively knew that water would be their salvation and hesitated not even a moment before plunging into the river.

That late afternoon we planned to eat and sleep until nighttime, than take off while the desert cooled off. Our best laid plans again crumbled. One of the Studebaker tires blew for no apparent reason except to mess up our best-intentioned plans. Buddy and Joe removed the wheel and headed for the nearest garage. I was rather glad I was a woman who could feign ignorance over changing a tire from a split rim in a hundred-degree heat at night.

Around midnight, a patched tire back on the pickup, bed sheet still flapping above the aspen pole and rawhide tied best-ever-stock-racks; we were on our way to California with no further disasters. Folks on the highway continued snapping pictures of the interesting contraption with two cowpokes in the cab sweating up a storm under their wide brimmed black cowboy hats. I remained my respectable distance behind the contraption.

We arrived at Rancho San Fernando Rey in time for the worst of the after-noon broil. "Damn, this place is hot," Joe complained as merciless heat waves reflected off the parched yellow hills.

At least the ranch manager provided us with a house on a ranch five miles from headquarters. "You can stay here," he apologized, "until the other house is ready." Apparently, no one had been in a hurry to clean out and ready our new ranch home.

We immediately fell in love with our temporary home. The cozy ranch home was furnished with Mexican tables, chairs and sideboards. The white frame house hid under peach and oak trees to escape the relentless California sun. The lovely and ancient Spanish land grant ranch nestled among giant oaks spreading their tremendous limbs over the barns and corrals. Pastures beyond the barns mean-dered toward a riverbed, fringed with aromatic bay trees. We turned Wolf and Smokey loose in the nearest pasture. They bucked and ran with great joy after escaping the old Studebaker and headed for the furthest reaches of the pasture with not one backward glance at the best-ever-stock-racks.

Life returned to normal for a few hours. We rested after our journey. The churning and droning of the Studebaker engine for the past three days had been silenced. Gone were the heavy fumes belched from its rusty tailpipe. Only the buzzing of flies permeated the blistering and lazy afternoon. The heaviness of worry as a constant companion on our journey miraculously transformed into hope as the evening breeze cooled the land. "This is it," I said, "This is home. Our dream job. Forever."

As soon as night blanketed a bronze and orange sunset, Buddy and Joe promptly poached a fat deer. We were hungry, poor and meat had not been fig-ured into our budget. The following weeks, we dined like royalty on deer steaks, deer roasts, deer sausage, deer soup and deer meatballs. That first week, I did not yet know that I would learn to spice the meat with coriander, garlic and pepper-corns because deer would be a steady diet. At least that first night on the new ranch we thought of ourselves as darned smart to feast on such fine meals for the price of one shell.

Three years later, the dream job disintegrated, we were ready to head back to Colorado, not exactly voluntarily, but because of too many differences between Joe and the foreman at Rancho San Fernando Rey. My cowboy husband, disenchanted that he hadn't got the foreman job, visualized greener fields. Goodbye California. Hello Colorado.

The green fields turned out white, not green. Joe found his next job at Parshall, Colorado. "Plenty of cattle. No farm work and we got us a good house," Joe reported after he talked to the foreman about the lovely amenities...

"We ain't going through that last hassle again," Joe announced that this move would be easier than the last one. Buddy remained in California and Joe sold the old Studebaker with the best-ever-stock-racks to another needy cowboy. The cowboy bought the pickup providing we would make him a real good deal. We did not have a problem with offering an attractive deal. I felt not in the least sorry that I would have to replace the Studebaker with another vehicle. We still owned the Chrysler convertible and had come up in society by buying a horse trailer. That still left us transporting our worldly belongings, having increased further in quantity. My search for transportation ended in Santa Barbara when I bought a 1959 Cadillac Couple De Ville for two hundred and fifty dollars. "Just look at this car," I bragged to Joe. "This is the biggest car on the road. It'll pull the horse trailer like it isn't back there."

"Yep, it looks like it'll pull anything," Joe agreed.

The Cadillac did not disappoint our expectation and pulled horse trailer with the horses, the dogs, the cats, the anvil and the saddles.

We were in high spirits and certain this trip would be free of problems because we knew all about moving by now. Did we not learn from the last journey? Just in case, we chose Raton instead of Wolf Creek pass.

After we crammed our worldly and non-worldly possessions the extra large size U-haul, Smokey and Wolf, by now seasoned travelers to many horse shows, jumped into the horse trailer. They probably thought this would be another short haul to a horse show.

Coach and Black Puppy, our two cow dogs, rode in the Cadillac with a certain pomposity after riding in the back of trucks and pickup beds. Klatz, our male Burmese cat and his sister Pewter with six kittens were stowed in a cage in the trailer's manger. The horses were not particularly perturbed while munching hay next to a brood of meowing kittens.

With past experience under our belt, we decided to forfeit sleep and cross the hot desert at night. We headed toward the fringes of the desert and rolled into the hellish open space of the Mojave, where snakes say goodnight at midnight and endless caravans of trucks haul ass over the speed limit and truckers their sights on the cool Rocky Mountains.

Obsessed to leave the desert behind us by morning, we too 'hauled ass' with our sights on the Rockies, but as midnight neared, mirages appeared, visions of feather beds and air conditioning intruded on my concentration, and each light whizzing by on the highway seemed to diffuse into confusing reflections. I signaled Joe to pull over at the first wide spot on the road. "I'm so tired," I complained, "I can't even see straight."

We decided to unload the horses, something we should have done hours ago. Joe untied Smokey through the escape hatch and Smokey more than willingly backed out of the trailer, anticipating feed and water. Once we cared for Smokey, Joe squeezed himself between the petition and Wolf to untie him as well. At that very instant, a huge rig screamed past our little caravan. The semi roared into a higher gear, shattering the steady hum of traffic. Wolf, most likely with nerves already on edge for riding through the night, reared in fright and, striking Joe with his forelegs, lunged on top of Joe. Joe ended up under Wolf's belly while Wolf reared and pawed with the fear of the unexpected. I heard a muffled cry for help.

"Get this horse off of me!"

With an instantaneous vision of a dead or maimed husband in the middle of the desert, I raced into the empty half of the trailer, heard the panicked cursing. "Damn, get him off of me." Wolf continued to bash his legs on the side and front of the trailer. My hands shook as I untied Wolf and pulled him backward. When I tied Wolf and returned to the rear of the trailer my worst fear had not materialized. Aside from bruises, Joe survived. For the second time in my Appaloosa's life, I briefly entertained equine homicide. Instead, I tied him to the trailer, fed him hay, grain, brought a pail of water and said a few choice words to him.

Since bad things happen in threes, that night was about to be such an example. An ill adventure never ends with just one incident. Because the cage had been placed in the manger on Wolf's side, it had received blows from Wolf's slashing hoofs. The story turned into a nightmare when we found the cage empty. All eight cats were nowhere in sight and escaped into the desert. Couldn't blame them for not sticking around for the grand finale.

At the stroke of midnight, we crossed the desert, calling, "Here kitty, here kitty, kitty!" The desert remained unresponsive within the cloak of night, the trucks continued to whine past and creosote bushes appeared like apparitions in flashlight beams.

"Klatz baby, Pewter, damn you, kitty, kitty, come here, you little #*!%^." Our flashlights beamed left, right, and back and forth, under creosote bushes and beside cactus and boulders. We finally found the cats huddled among rocks and all too willing to return to their rescuers.

After the cat search, Joe had to complete a quick fix-it job on the demolished cat cage while I stashed the cats in the car until he completed the repair job. The cats safely in their repaired cage, the dogs watered, the horses closing their eyes, we carried our bedroll to a spot with the least amount of cactus. I slept amidst rocks, oblivious to rattlesnake dens or tarantulas. Big rigs rolled past the rest of the night, but we tuned out their roar and their incessant growl of gear changes and ignored rocks jabbing us through the sleeping bag. In the morning, we would leave the desert behind and behold the white capped Rocky Mountains. We would soon be home. I looked forward to life on a lovely spread in the midst of the Rocky Mountains with elk and deer to hunt, columbines in green meadows and riding in country that God created when he felt especially artistic.

We clung to our lofty expectation. The final part of our journey was nothing short of an arctic misadventure. Parshall, as we learned on the day of arrival, is the coldest spot in the lower states, giving Alaska's sub zero temperatures a run for first place. Parshall was indecently cold. Weather reports conveniently forgot to mention temperatures lest they frighten away tourists from nearby ski areas. The boss forgot to mention that over the telephone.

The soaring Rockies that imprisoned below-zero temperatures surrounded our imaginary green pastures in Parshall. Ranches hid under tons of ice and snow, with ice in the clouds, ice on cars, ice on water tanks, ice on haystacks, ice in the water lines and ice frosting our faces. Our cats and dogs were never far from the front door, begging to become house pets. Although our dogs were seldom allowed in the house, their pleading eyes were enough to allow them to curl up on the mud porch.

Joe and I got up at seven in the morning to feed cattle. Rising earlier was useless as the dark starry skies covered a frozen wasteland that would only respond to sunlight, and then grudgingly. We dressed in survival clothing, costing a bundle that had not been budgeted into Joe's meager income. Snowmobile boots with felt liners, Eddie Bauer down jackets rated for climbing Mount Everest, extra insulated mittens and knit face masks were standard gear for the feeding routine. The ranch owned one Clydesdale, a sweet old man, whom we hitched to the sled with wide iron runners. Within a few days we learned iron runners freeze to the ground once dusk sweeps sub-zero air over the day's softened ice and snow. We used a space heater the size of a jet engine to de-ice the sled runners.

De-icing was the first part of the feeding routine. Part two included consisted of driving the sled to the haystack piled as high as a house with loose hay, surrounded by tall elk fencing. Breathing into our knitted facemask was vital unless we wanted our lungs frozen. Part three entailed climbing the massive stack covered with a crust of ice. Joe used a pitchfork to loosen the hay underneath the ice and cussed into knit facemask that muffled his choice words.

My activity during part three included waiting for Joe to throw a mountain of hay onto the sled. Winds in the open meadow increased the temperature to seventy-below zero. The cold bit like a rabid dog into my face. Hands and toes hurt enough to cry. To save myself from the worst of the pain, I hid under the Clydesdale's head and soaked up his warm breath.

Part four consisted of feeding the cows as I drove the sled homeward. Joe threw off bundles of hay. When we finished feeding, the morning sun glistened off blue ice crystals and the lowland pastures transformed into a glittering and blazing silver blanket.

Home waited with heat cranked up to eighty degrees. When we removed our facemask, nose, cheeks and chin unthawed and turned red. Toes started to tingle. While Joe unhitched the Clydesdale, I cooked breakfast with hot chocolate sinfully rich with cream from the resident Jersey cow. The pungent smell of chocolate filled the kitchen, mountains of whipped cream topped the hot chocolate, and the first sip while sausages sizzled in the skillet erased all thoughts of our frozen and painful morning. Calories did not matter during energy consuming days. We devoured a vulgar amount of calories and remained as slim as a young aspen tree.

When temperatures dropped to forty-five below during the day, pipes froze and I had to wash the dinner dishes in the bathtub for weeks on end. Our car had to be unfrozen with the jet-size space heater whenever we wanted to drive someplace in the morning before the high altitude sun could work on a frozen engine. Even in a closed shed, the car could not escape the clutches of killer frost.

Sometimes the sun managed to win for a day or two and then we almost spotted the surface of the road. The corrals turned into a pond of mud, freezing again during the night. Before spring melted the ground into a sea of mud surrounding the house, outbuildings and barns, and transformed pastures into green and spongy fields, we moved out of our frozen hellhole to lower altitudes.

When Joe found a job on a feedlot in Sedgewick on the Colorado plains, far away from the mountains, we packed with renewed expectation and hope. "A farmhouse with eleven rooms, and lots of riding in the feed yard," he bragged about this new dream job. "Also a chance to get promoted to foreman. The new boss promised." Compared to Parshall, Sedgewick seemed like heaven. Joe's cowboy boots were exchanged with the snowmobile boots that squatted by the stove with liners removed to dry for the next day's work. I knew that a cowboy who can't wear his boot is a cowboy with itchy feet and hankered to slip those boots back into a set of stirrups.

As the pipes to the Parshall kitchen grudgingly thawed, this offer seemed too lucrative to turn down. I hoped that this would be Joe's chance to hang his hat, wear his boots and uncurl his rope. Thinking about another move, some nights the past intruded. What if we never find the dream job where we can save for a place of our own? The thoughts were too unsettling. I refused to allow them to intrude on my dreams.

We scraped together the needed dollars and moved during the tail end of a snowstorm chasing out of the Rockies. The Chrysler pulled the U-haul and the faithful Caddie pulled the horse trailer. The move was uneventful except for negotiating 12,500 foot Berthoud pass with treacherous icy hairpin curves descending to the eastern side of the Rockies. I shifted to first gear and descended Berthoud pass at a crawl, noting a semi that slid off the road, saved from plunging over rocky cliffs by a stand of trees clinging to the sheer precipice of the mountain. Our horses appeared to sense the precarious drive, cooperating throughout the trip without stomping or shifting weight. At the bottom of the pass, I again breathed normal and drove endless miles of monotonous prairie to our new home.

In our haste to escape our icy hellhole, we did not investigate our New World. We did not know about the flies, howling wind, footwork instead of horse work, vicious thunderstorms, dust and monotony. The flies were as thick as molasses clinging on each screen in all eleven rooms of the house. The screens were supposed to keep them out, but they laid eggs and in no time, the house inside buzzed with flies as plump as raisins. The windows remained shut most of the time, not just to keep out flies, but to avoid the fragrance of the feed lot permeating every room of the farm house. The smells of molasses mixed with manure and grain alcohol from fermenting corn impregnated the air for miles.

The wind never quit, and blew morning, afternoon, and evenings. On a good day, it blew twenty mile an hour. On a bad day, it blew fifty mile an hour. Everything on the Colorado prairie was bent permanently by the wind. Hearing was impaired because of the howl and whistle of the wind and when talking to folks they said "ay?" if you didn't shout above the howl of the wind. Horses held their heads down, the trees grew crooked, the fences leaned away from the prevailing wind, dust devils played in fields and corrals, and folks walked everywhere stooped over. They had forgotten to walk upright during rare moments when the wind did not blow. They stooped just the same. Young and old looked as if they had an advanced case of osteoporosis.

Worst of all, Joe did not ride the way he pictured a cowboy should ride in a feed lot. The owner never rode horses and expected Joe to accomplish herding cattle on foot.

"Whoever heard of running around on foot like a bunch of farmers?" Joe grumbled at the end of the day. "The *&^%! don't know what horses are for?"

The Eddie Bauer anti-freezing outfits were exchanged for mud crusted jeans and rubber over-boots. After a rain, fishing waders might have been more appropriate. The cowboy boots leaned against the wall of the mud porch, reminding Joe to search for greener pastures. Joe and I rode as much as we could get away with when sorting cattle, accompanied by the boss's spurious comments. "You know, people can do a lot better on foot."

The owner plowed around the muddy pens in his rubber boots while Joe stepped on his horse. "Yes sir," Joe forced a polite smile to the anti-horse comments. We kept our mouth shut and our thoughts to ourselves. We also kept the news that we'd be a family to ourselves or the boss might have objected when I rode my horse in the pens. Joe said farmers were like that. They might approve of the wife a tractor, but not a horse.

We stuck it out for the rest of the year, enduring a mean spirited winter because there was no money in the kitty for moving. The prairie winter did not bring as much snow as in the Rockies but when winter blew onto the vast stretches of the flat land, blizzards obscured everything. Roads were impassable for days and mountains of snowdrifts blocked snowplows. Fields and corrals transformed into sludge. The wind blustered relentlessly, roared through clothing and into the cracks of the old house. With the arrival of spring, the feed yard turned into an ocean of mud no less than one and some days, two feet deep. Dried mud coated the horse's bellies, crept past the knee on jeans, clung to overshoes like black glue and turned the mud porch into its namesake. Joe continued to grumble, curse farmers, mud and wind. The prime side of beef we butchered could not make up for the cantankerous prairie life.

Again, we read the Western Livestock Journal for ads advertising real cowboy jobs. We tolerated the flies; the acrid feed lot odor, the wind and waited for something good to appear in the help wanted section month after month. Joe grew restless. I wandered through my eleven flyspecked rooms, hoping the baby would be born someplace with sweeter air. Joe itched all over and in desperation called his favorite dude ranch. "We're going back," he hollered, "I'm gonna rodeo again, and I'm on a horse again, instead of walking in mud like a damn farmer."

"Where will we live?" I asked with a bit of caution since the last time we lived in a room until Mr. Snell built a tiny two-room house. Soon we would have a family and needed a decent home.

Joe was too excited to think about my priorities as a new mother with a baby. "They got a decent house. It'll be nice. I'll retire there," he assured me while he already imagined riding in the weekly rodeo. "Yea, sure," I* mumbled and attempted to ignore my skepticism yet the tingle of excitement shoved doubts into the background. Knowing we could finally move out of fly heaven seemed like winning the lottery, or winning a ticket to the Garden of Eden. We packed again.

"This is it, little bride," Joe promised, "the last time we move."

We remained at Paradise Ranch for five glorious years before the next journey to another place that would positively be the final homestead. When Paradise Ranch closed its doors forever because the era of big dude ranches passed, we once again packed boxes, once again had to figure out how to haul horses, dogs and cats with a new addition of two little crumb-crunchers.

After the bankruptcy of Paradise Ranch, the court allowed us to live at the ranch until everything was sold off and the grandest of all dude ranches turned into a ghost town. No more harness jingling, no more thundering from a hundred horse's hoofs, the squeaky wheels of the stagecoaches, clouds of dust during a wild and wooly rodeo, the sweet smell of hey in two hundred mangers and rides into the untamed and precarious back country of Pikes Peak. When our halcyon years ended at Paradise Ranch, we rented a home nearby and hoped for a dream job in California. Colorado was passé. California beckoned.

After carefree years at Paradise Ranch, we were again cast into poverty, worry, and the unemployment line. When the ranch closed, we lost our pine-paneled home, barns and corrals for our horses, and the paychecks. We were now parents of two little crumb-crunchers, and Joe had to swallow his pride and accept a job in a mine in Cripple Creek. Instead of a cowboy hat, he wore a hard hat, and instead of cowboy boots, he wore lace-up clodhoppers. He was unhappy as hell as a miner. We could barely hang onto our dreams as I waited in food stamp lines and applied for reduced utility bills.

The arrival of the Western Livestock Journal became the most important day of the week. As the clodhoppers squeezed Joe's feet and the hard hat refused to feel like a cowboy hat, Joe became less picky about finding the perfect cowboy job. We checked out ads that would have been ignored if Joe had not been desperate to get back on a horse. After a winter of searching, we were ready to move someplace besides California. Wyoming, Montana, California, or New Mexico? As long as there were good horses, no farming and a decent place to hang a hat.

The ad that finally sparked Joe's interest appeared after months of checking out false hopes. "A million acre ranch in Northern California, prefer a cowboy with experience who could take over as foreman in the future. Needs to know horses and cattle. Remodeled modern ranch home, close to town, shopping and schools."

"That's got to be it," Joe announced. The salary was the usual mediocre shabby cowboy wage, but the promise of a foremen promotion seemed like a good enough deal. Joe and I agreed this might be the place. We imagined a riding and hunting on a million acres. "You know I gotta ride every day on a place like that," Joe convinced himself. I imagined a modern ranch home and a chance to ride, rope and train a horse or two for barrel racing.

Our return move to California seemed a vacation compared to earlier moves because we hired a moving van. The expense was beyond a cowboy salary, but we figured we deserved a break. We still had to haul the horses, the dogs and cats. With the little cowpokes added, the moving van decision seemed the right one. Never mind the van cost our savings. We were on top of the world and somewhat smug. A huge cattle ranch. A riding job. A modern home. What more could a cowboy want? We still owned the convertible and the Cadillac and either could pull our brand new Stidham horse trailer. We were proud of ourselves for being wise enough to move in style and agreed that this move would be a breeze.

After the moving van left us with an empty house, we crawled out of our sleeping bags at an indecent early hour, loaded our two horses and the dogs, cats, kids, their toys and were off once more for the far West and greener pastures. Joe pulled the horse trailer while I bundled the kids in the Cadillac. The crumb-crunchers were old enough to feel excited by the new adventure. Did they inherit the cowboy spirit?

Joe led the way while I followed, with a thermos of coffee on the front seat. We cruised along highway twenty-five, from Colorado to Las Vegas, New Mexico. No problem! Until we arrived in Las Vegas. My Cadillac missed and coughed and as soon as I spotted a sign for a Cadillac dealer, I tried to alert Joe. I flashed my lights, honked the horn, but Joe happily sped through a green light, turned right to follow the road out of Las Vegas, and disappeared. The thought of driving to California on my own was unpleasant, but at least I found the Cadillac dealer. As soon as the hood of the Cadillac was up, a brilliant idea occurred to me. Why not, I reasoned, call the sheriff and ask him to intercept my husband? "I have a slight problem." I confided to the officer.

"Yes ma'm?"

"You see, I lost my husband. We're on our way to California. He wears a big black Stetson and drives a convertible with a horse trailer. And I'm stuck at the Cadillac garage!" I added.

To my relief, the sheriff seemed cooperative. "He doesn't know where you are?"

"No, we got separated. Could you find him?"

Every Las Vegas deputy sheriff cooperated on the lost cowboy search. Within an hour, I spotted the black and white police cruiser and in tow, a convertible driven by a cowboy in a big black hat.

After replacing a sparkplug wire we were on our way. On this journey, unlike the others, we spent the night in luxury in a motel room. The youngest cowpoke was too young to appreciate the Holiday Inn, but the oldest splashed and played in the children's pool. I too luxuriated in such extravaganza that we seldom experienced. Clean rooms, a pool, a sauna, dinner in a restaurant instead of campground grub and sleeping under the stars.

Finding overnight accommodations for the horses of course preceded each overnight stay. Fairgrounds turned out to be the most reasonable and available accommodations. We brought along a chain and locked the corral gate just in case some enterprising person thought that our horses might supplement their income.

The next day passed without problems. We felt we had the trip by the tail until we changed vehicles and in some unnamed, unremembered highway town I smartly followed Joe making a U-turn and turned too soon. The horse trailer tires stuck against the curb of the median is no disaster as long as it is not rush hour. A long line of traffic formed behind the horse trailer. Horns honked. Drivers leaned out of their windows. Backing up was impossible, since the next car had followed the trailer with a few inches to spare. The next car also played bumper cars and so on down the line. Cars continued to honk, a few drivers shouted, "Hey, get her going," as I sat in my Cadillac and figured if people were too stupid to back up, I would simply sit there and wait. The situation appeared hopeless. Jim or Fred or Judy at the end of the line couldn't figure out they had to back up for the rest of the twenty cars in front of them. At first, everyone just sat there, glaring at the dumb country hick with the trailer. Eventually a car way back managed to pull out and everyone else backed up. Finally, I maneuvered the trailer away from the curb, no easy feat because the trailer faced west and the Cadillac faced south.

From New Mexico, we drove into the great Mojave Desert. The last two trips through the Mojave held memories we preferred to forget. We were determined to rewrite our page of history.

Few major highways transcend the Mojave, straight and mesmerizing and one mile exactly like the last fifty miles and the next fifty miles. During this monotonous transition, I pulled the horse trailer and Joe followed. On one of those interminably long stretches, a semi rig appeared anxious to pass. I thought little of it, as truck drivers usually pushed their eight wheelers far over the speed limit, and allowed him to pass, courteously pulling onto the wide paved shoulder. The semi sped up next to my car, but did not pass. He downshifted and stayed right there, in my lane. I decelerated to allow him to pass and move on. The semi also decelerated, crowding my Cadillac onto the shoulder of the road. By now I figured a sadistic trucker was bored and played a game, the kind you see in disaster movies. I slowed further after I spotted a bridge in the distance. The truck also slowed. By now, I realized I had become his pawn in a dangerous game. I stepped on the gas to get ahead, but the truck also sped up, ramming it into another gear. I slowed again to stop before the bridge with its railing jutting out into the shoulder of the road. In the meantime, Joe had figured out the game when I spotted him pulling into the opposite lane, his left hand out the window, pointing his .44 Magnum at the truck driver's cab. The .44 turned into a magic wand. Within seconds, the trucker roared past my car, shifting gears as he pushed the big rig into high gear. We stopped at the next truck stop, and the next one, hoping to find the trucker and give him a piece of our mind, but the truck had disappeared. We figured that trucker stepped on his accelerator and kept right on going. He may have had thoughts of playing games or running me off the road, but he obviously decided he had better not deal a mean looking cowboy in a big black hat and a .44 Magnum.

After the incident in the desert, no more mishaps occurred. We cruised past the edge of the arid Mojave, past checkered farm fields of the San Joaquin Valley, and finally to the Siman Newman Ranch.

Within five minutes we discovered the wonderful modern ranch home was not wonderful, but a decrepit migrant shack. A week later, the wonderful cowboy job was also not wonderful.

The day we arrived in the San Joaquin Valley, spring felt as oppressive and dusty as summer. The simmering heat combined with thousands of sprinklers from the fertile valley drove the humidity to sweaty highs. The foreman's attitude was oppressive, the working conditions oppressive, and the social life oppressive.

In six months, we moved again toward less oppressive pastures in Southern California.

We considered the move from Gustine in Northern California to Santa Ynez in Southern California insignificant compared to other journeys across endless stretches of the West. The flight from the oppressive Hartford ranch to Happy Canyon Ranch in the bucolic Santa Ynez Valley was a short day's drive. Who could complain? With only a few pennies in our pocket, we moved.

With pennies in our pocket, traveling in style had come to an abrupt end. Back to the longest, highest, widest U-haul. We stuffed, pushed and bent everything into the trailer. Our beautiful convertible had been traded for a sensible pickup designated to pull the horse trailer. Naturally, this journey did not occur without a disaster. The sensible pickup engine threatened to boil with each bump in the road. With my eyes glued to the temperature gage, I floored the pickup and roared at ninety mile an hour south. The sensible pickup arrived at Happy Canyon Ranch with an intact engine and horses unaware of the wild race to our new home.

Happy Canyon Ranch appeared, soothing to the eye and heart after the harshness and injustice of the San Joaquin Valley. "This time," Joe promised, "we got the right place. This is it."

I gazed from the kitchen window past the apricot tree to the weathered barn and the live oaks shading a white washed fence surrounding the horse paddock. How long ago had it been when my hopes and dreams were soaring along with Joe's to a place of our own? I still believed in my cowboy. We settled into our new home on this green patch of nirvana in Happy Canyon. There were fat cattle, game to hunt, good horses and a boss who understood cowboys. The two crumb-crunchers played in a green yard fringed by daffodils in the spring and roses in the summer with night blooming jasmine drifting into the open windows during long summer evenings. The boys rode ponies. Cattle drives, roping and barbecues occupied weekends. Joe left every morning to tend to chores with a happy heart of a satisfied cowboy.

3

Horses and Critters

A Hibernian sage once wrote there are three things a man never forgets: The girl of his early youth, a devoted teacher, and a great horse.

I was privileged to have owned one great horse, although I have owned and ridden untold others, horses ranging from darned good to darned bad.

Horses were my panacea in a cowboy world that guaranteed nothing. Their powerful stride, the wind in my face, the sweet smell of their coat, a subtle neigh to say hello, the adrenaline rush of a wild race, and the height from which I could look down at the world were the balm and the magic potion in my life.

Paradise Guest Ranch below the grand Pikes Peak presented the most resplendent and diversified opportunities with horses that any cowboy or cowgirl could dream about. There were gentle nags, smart and nimble quarter horses, racy long legged equines with thoroughbred breeding, lumbering draft horses, horses that loved people and horses that just as soon kick human heads into the next county. As the foreman's wife, my privileges included choosing any horse I desired from the hundreds at the ranch.

Sweet Pea, a bundle of compact dynamite had become one of my favorite horses. As nimble as a wildcat, always on edge and anxious, her sudden burst of speed could set a rider back in the saddle if not ready for her jackrabbit start. She was my Ferrari sports car who could outperform the big cars and run circles around them with boundless enthusiasm. Her dainty legs belied her stamina, and her body with well formed rounded muscles hinted of a powerhouse despite her diminutive size. Her coat gleamed like the color of bittersweet chocolate frosting. During her frequent and sudden panic attacks nothing but gravity helped a rider stay on her back. She abhorred strange objects, snorted through flared nostrils, danced, and attempted to jump out of her own skin when something appeared strange or dangerous. As far as Sweet Pea was concerned, there were too many spooky objects in the world. They never got less spooky no matter how many times she passed something she decided would attack her. She loved speed.

Whips and spurs were unnecessary. She offered every ounce of energy anytime she noticed an opportunity to turn up the heat. I challenged other riders with tall, fast and leggy thoroughbred type horses. "You wanna race?" I asked, looking up at the rider.

They looked down at me. "Sure, but I got me one fast horse, that little mare ain't no match." The super confident cowboy would have to eat his words. Sweet Pea won against super-sized horse with the meanest reputation for speed. She won barrel races without blinking an eye.

Sweet Pea was a Paradise Ranch horse and belonged to the dude string, but her peppery disposition eliminated her as a dude horse. I claimed her as one of my wrangling horses with no complaints from the boss. Since my cowboy husband was the barn boss, I could claim any horse I fancied. Sweet Pea gained privileged status among the dude horses and we treated her like a queen. She resided in her own corral and did not have to compete for hay and grain with the hundreds of other horses. A sturdy pole fence separated Sweet Pea from the Brahma bull pasture. More important, the fence also separated me from the bulls.

One fine day, I discovered Sweet Pea missing from her corral. I checked the gate, but it was locked. I thought perhaps someone played a joke and hid her someplace on the ranch. The wranglers always played jokes on each other, but no one admitted any shenanigans. I checked every possible hiding place on the ranch and turned up nothing. After searching as if we were looking for Easter eggs, Joe and I walked back to the corral to figure out how this little horse might have turned up missing. About to give up, we happened to look toward the Brahma bull pasture. There she stood, eyes closed, as content as a bee in a flower, resting next to one of the Brahma bulls that happened to be the most massive of two dozen Brahman in the rodeo string. Both bull and horse seemed quite comfortable, hide to hide, dozing away the afternoon.

"No way, Jose," I objected when Joe expected me to catch Sweet Pea.

"She's your horse," he tried again while two dozen Brahman checked us out with beady eyes…

"So," I asked, "you going to get her?"

"Sure." Joe sounded resigned. He sprinted into action, but none of the bulls offered to challenge his presence.

A few days later, Sweet Pea turned up missing again, this time I knew where to look and found her again with the same massive bull, both contentedly leaning up against each other.

"You think one of our wranglers is playing a joke on us and puts her in here?" Joe contemplated.

Again, no one owned up to the prank. The mysterious transfer from corral to bull pasture continued periodically. We always found Sweet Pea with the same bull.

After playing detective for a few more weeks, we finally noticed tell tale signs. The bottom pole of her corral seemed high enough off the ground for a horse to fit under the railing if Sweet Pea lay on her side. We finally figured out that she had figured out that if she flopped on her flanks and pushed with her legs she could slide to the other side of the corral. Joe attached another pole to the bottom of the corral, but we both felt like traitors interfering in a bull-horse love affair.

Sweet Pea remained one of my favorite horses and since Joe was the foreman, she was my private horse and no one got to ride her unless I approved. None of the wranglers ever asked to ride her. Their reasons were obvious. "Hell, I ain't ridin' this crazy horse. She's plain nuts." They could tolerate a horse that bucked but they objected to a horse that twirled, danced and bolted. A bucking horse gave a cowboy hero status; a twirling and spooking horse didn't do much for their ego or admiration from others.

One of Sweet Pea's most appreciable attributes was her size. I could get on her back without excessive stretching and climbing. Under five foot two inches, I often found myself in a fix when mounting tall horses. The stirrups were simply too high up for my short legs. Since super tight jeans were the fashion, they were not designed to stretch over the knee. Encased in non-stretchable jeans with stirrups as high as my shoulder, mounting a horse resulted in an interesting task. Add a horse refusing to stand still and climbing into the saddle could turn into a critical event. With Sweet Pea, I was able to jump on her back regardless that she attempted to race to some distant place before I reached her back. To her, the rider's weight in the stirrup became the bell on the racetrack.

Other horses were another story. I used fences, ditches, placing them down slope, pulling their head around to the side to restrict that predictable bolt away from the rider. Pulling the bridle toward the rider often caused further problems of swinging the rear end away. The horse played a game of moving in a circle until I pushed the horse next to a fence or tree. With certain disreputable horses, I lengthened my stirrups, then adjusted them once astride. Condescending cowboys offered to help the little lady on the horse which, out of pride, I declined.

"Here, let me help you," was a common solicitation. I figured some of those helpful gestures were an excuse to hug my waist and I always rejected the self-serving offers. Sometimes, the horse won and I lost. He moved sideways at just the right time or charged into the wild blue yonder as if leading Custer's last battle. A few horses stood rooted to the ground and endured my efforts at climbing on their backs the traditional way.

Snoopy was bar-none the tallest horse I have ever owned. I had to stand on my toes and stretch my arm over my head to reach the top of his withers with my fingertips. Through sheer desperation, I taught Snoopy to stand patiently in a ditch or on the downside of a hill while I climbed on. Snoopy's extraordinary height elicited bets from cowboys that I couldn't get on him. I heard plenty of jokes about the discrepancy of size between rider and horse.

"Here, let me give you a hand." They offered, but I just hitched up my pant legs, thanked them politely, and headed for a ditch or a fence.

Snoopy's silver mane and tail set off a dark chocolate brown coat. Black stockings and white socks completed a striking picture. His unusual and flashy color drew my attention and I thought it would be fun to own such a huge, powerful, flashy horse. I always did have a thing about sitting way up on a horse and looking down on people. Snoopy did not elicit love at first sight. In hindsight, the purchase had been more ego than horse sense.

"That horse is crazy." Joe commented, ignoring that had selected plenty of crazy ones for me from the Paradise string. "If you buy him, don't ask me to ride him," he threatened.

Riding him was not unlike riding a container of TNT. Any noise, any movement caused Snoopy to blow up, lunge, run, whirl or twist. Much as my little Sweet Pea, but his size made up two Sweet Peas. Snoopy's strength surpassed that of the average horse. Perhaps no one wanted to ride him because it felt as if the rider sat up there for the ride and if Snoopy decided he could do with his rider as he pleased. The sense of sheer power accompanied a sense helplessness on every ride. Snoopy required a calm rider with lots of finesse and a quiet voice with good intuition to contain his explosive behaviors. Most cowboys lacked the patience.

Joe's refrained from further comments when I bought my monster sized horse. I think he felt that if I was crazy enough to want the horse, I could figure out how to handle him. He also stuck with his original threat. "Don't expect me to ride that horse." I learned that when I needed help with Snoopy I was on my own.

I rode Snoopy throughout the winter in mild and balmy California without major mishaps. "You're lucky, mark my word, that horse is bad news." Joe advised more than once.

On a fine spring day, we were invited to Monty Robert's Flag is Up racehorse farm to take part in a yearly day at the races, a charity affair to raise money for the Santa Barbara symphony.

The day began promising. A vibrant ocean breeze brushed horses and riders, cooling the sweat horses worked up by sensing the excitement. Spectators gathered in suits and ties, ladies showing off their Sunday finery under fancy hats, sipping champagne, surveying the entries with a skeptical eye for speed or clues for picking the winners. Soon the action started. A flurry of last minute betting, the bugler playing the traditional tune and the familiar announcement: "They're off."

During the first races, thoroughbreds thundered to the homestretch, each stride cheered on by spectators with champagne glasses. The harness races followed with the clink-clink-clink of harness and hoofs pounding the sand. Even a mule race brought feverish betting and cheering. Finally, it was our turn. A relay race. Four teams of three riders each, with equal distance to cover on the track. I was in the third and final lap, riding my 1,700 pounds of dynamite, his muscles quivering in anticipation. I rode to my position, checked out the distance in which the baton could be passed. Perhaps fifty yards. One had to be careful to get a firm grip on the baton before racing out of the boundary. I heard the bugle, the announcer's singsong voice: "And they are off." The butterflies in my stomach fluttered away. Time to get on with the business of winning. My partner passed the baton to the second one without losing stride. My second partner raced toward me, ahead of other horses, gaining a slight lead, leaning into the curve at the quarter mile marker.

Good, I thought, we have a chance to win. The horses in my heat were beginning to show nervousness with the approaching riders. A black horse in the number three position pulled at the bit in a frenzy, leaping forward and sideways. I checked my position. Once more, I checked the other three horses in my lap. They rode ahead perhaps ten to fifteen yards. I checked the gap between the rail and my number one position, leaving enough room for my partner to ride in between. Then I glanced backward, watching my partner as he approached, his horse stretched out, flying down the track. Time to start galloping, not too fast yet, but I knew I had to get my horse into smooth motion. Unexpectedly Snoopy lunged and for a brief moment, demanded all of my attention to slow him down.

In the same breath, my powerful horse's body snatched around by a horse plowing into him. He struggled to regain his balance, leaped into the air but his hind feet had been knocked out from under him. Flung out of the saddle, the jolt catapulted me into the air, landing hard on the track, falling clear of my horse. I felt no pain, only thankfulness that I avoided falling under this huge horse. Unable to move, I lay flat on my back on the sand and felt confused. Where were the other horses? Where was Snoopy? The world around me a blur, I could not see if my horse was all right. Perhaps he had recovered and bolted from the chaos. A gray shape, I thought it was gray, or perhaps the dust played tricks, raced toward my prone body. I was not sure if the shape was a horse. The shape looked like a chest, long legs, looming large, larger, nearly on top of me. I talked myself out of the thought that this was a horse, running straight for where I lay motionless. Perhaps it was an illusion?

I felt helpless, but not frightened. The shape would surely disappear, or stop. My attempts at focusing on the blurry shape shattered with a harsh blow to the side of my head. The blurry world turned black. I floated in a void, silent and very dark. For the most fleeting of moment, I felt frightened. What was happening? Within that moment, the world became peaceful. After the black world faded, I saw my husband leaning over me. The sky above was full of faces looking down. Someone threw a cloth over my head. "Keep the dust out," I heard. With one hand, I pulled the cloth off. Did they think I was dead?

I felt at peace, content to lie on my back. A blurry shape in a black suit talked to me. He said something about being a doctor. He made me move my legs and arms. "Good, good," he repeated, "she's not paralyzed." A voice said to get me up on my feet, but my legs refused to cooperate. It felt numb. Slowly, my husband and the doctor helped me stand. I tried to look for my horse, but there were too many people milling around the track. "Is Snoopy ok?" No one answered. The first waves of pain gripped my neck, my head, and my back.

One of my race partners bent down. I noticed the concern and tried to smile. A forced crooked smile, but yes, I'm ok, I mumbled. The paramedics were already at the track. Deliberately, step by slow step, they walked me to the ambulance when I waved away the gurney. On the way, we passed a dead horse. A broken back, someone said and pointed to the owner of the dead horse leaning on the back of the ambulance, crying. For now, I allowed everyone else to take care of me, do the thinking and worrying for me.

A news film produced the answer why the accident happened. One of the other horses in my heat and ahead of my horse had spun sideways and placed himself in my horse's way. Another horse lost his cool, running and slamming into my horse, catapulting him backward. The rest of the horses racing toward us could not stop in time to avoid the disaster. Seven horses collided, four riders ended up with serous injuries, and one horse was dead. My head sustained a concussion when the gray horse jumped over my prone body and kicked me in the head. My tailbone was cracked, a vertebrae bruised, but the injuries healed.

I rode as soon as the pain subsided and was surprised that I did not carry the fear of another accident. The accident taught me that fear is only what one conjures up as fearful. Fear is absent during the moments of a catastrophe. I had felt no panic and no fear but for a fleeting moment. I figured that the mind denies fear to take over during the worst moments.

"Hell, you better get rid of that horse," the cowboys advised, but I did not blame Snoopy, and continued to ride him despite continued negative comments.

"He did what I had asked," I defended my big lummox of a horse. By early summer, I healed and the headaches disappeared. Then the next incident happened with Snoopy.

Joe, his boss Lance and two other cowboys gathered a herd of cattle. The mother cows and steers strung out along a trail snaking beside a narrow carved arroyo about as deep as the height of two horses. As usual, Snoopy showed his impatience when he neared the barn. He had visions of not sugarplums but a feed bag of grain dancing in his head. His muscles tightened, he started his jittery dance left and right when I refused to allow him to dash for the barn. He drummed his feet on the narrow path and suddenly slipped on the soft sandy edge of the arroyo. I felt his rear quarter following. Within a heartbeat, I had to decide on my course of action to save my hide. My first thought was to avoid going down there with him and within a second, I swung my foot out of my stirrup. Just as the rest of Snoopy slid over the edge, I stepped off. My survival instincts saved me that day from being mangled by a horse that outweighed me seventeen to one. As Snoopy disappeared into the arroyo, I sat on the edge, watching him flip over backward, crash saddle first into the bottom and with grunts and heaves, righting his thrashing bulk in the narrow ravine. I avoided thinking about what might have happened had I gone down with him.

Joe of course seized the moment to make a point about Snoopy being an unsafe horse. "Get rid of the S.O.B. before it's too late."

The cowboys just shook their head. "That horse is crazy."

"I wouldn't ride a horse like that," Lance said as he stuffed a wad of tobacco into his cheek.

I sold Snoopy sometime after the arroyo incident. The parent's of a little girl no bigger than a button, bought Snoopy. I warned the parents that Snoopy was like riding a package of TNT or dynamite, but they did not have the heart to say no to their little girl's longing looks. I missed the intense power I felt when I rode Snoopy, but I did not miss Snoopy. We never developed an affectionate relationship.

When we moved to Paradise Ranch for the second time, Joe bought a magnificent quarter horse with a silken red coat glistening like polished copper, a head chiseled like an artist's sculpture, and a glossy red mane and tail. We named him

Arrow because he was all speed and smoothness. He moved like oil on ice, fluid and quicker than a striking rattlesnake. Smarter than the average cowboy, Arrow belonged to the Mensa group of equines. The barn crew at Paradise Ranch avoided riding a horse with a higher IQ than their own. They preferred to play it safe. None of them relished riding a horse that knew how to buck off those who bragged that no horse could ever buck them off. Arrow would destroy a reputation with one good snap of his back. He chose unexpected moments when he knew the rider paid attention to something else. Zap, Arrow's head disappeared between his forelegs. He snapped his back like a whip and before the rider figured out the answer to two and two, he sailed in a great arc over Arrow's head.

Arrow dumped me once. I shot from the saddle as if I had been placed in a slingshot. His hind legs cracked like a whip, his back snapped and his head, between his legs, touched his belly. The incident lasted one or two seconds. Aside from my pride, I wasn't hurt and since no one watched the scenario, I kept it a secret.

"Finally got you, huh?" The remarks would have been said with glee.

I made it a point to learn Arrow's subtle signals when he contemplated bucking, waiting for me to divert my attention to something else. An ear pointed back, his nostrils slightly flared, an insignificant twitch of muscles were red flags. I thought I knew his every twitch and could prevent disaster except for that early morning when he had been cold and itched to buck. He had pretended to be subservient and cooperative, waiting for me to buy into his act until I let down my guard.

Now and then, he was straightforward about his need to buck and the bucking seemed for pure joy instead of intentionally dumping the rider. He loved charging up a hill in the mountains, and at the top of the hill he snatched his head from the rider's grasp and planted it between his forelegs for the pure joy of life. For good measure, Arrow whistled through his flared nostrils once he crested a hill, pretending he was a stud calling his harem.

Arrow almost dumped me a second time at our weekly rodeo. I rode him to post the colors and carried a heavy American flag. During Paradise Ranch rodeos, the colors were posted at a dead run. Spectators loved the display of speed, thundering hoofs and clouds of dust, the flapping of heavy flags, and the creaking and groaning of wagons thundering through the arena. To avoid a disaster, I shortened my reins considerably in case Arrow decided on a sneak attack. During a dead run around the arena, he managed to stick his head between his forelegs when I relaxed the reins, although not as far between his legs as usual, which probably saved me from a flying leap. I figured I couldn't stay on him if he bucked more than a twice. Holding on to the heavy flag prevented me from grabbing for leather and saving myself. I needed one hand to control the little devil and one to hold on to the horn, but dropping the flag seemed anti-American. My mind raced back and forth with the two choices. Hit the dirt, or let the flag hit the dirt. I finally decided that the old red, white and blue could withstand a beating more than I could. The embarrassment of being dumped in front of a thousand spectators was not appealing. I dropped the flag and in the nick of time, managed to pull Arrow's head up where it belonged. Someone raced to pick up the flag, I grabbed it and we completed our circuit. The spectators thought it was a great act.

As Arrow aged, he developed splints in his legs and appeared to be in pain under the weight of an adult. His working days were over and the itch to buck diminished. We found a home with a little girl whose parents promised that only their five-year-old could ride him around the home pasture. Arrow must have decided he needn't buck at all with a little five-year-old and seemed happy to carry her around the home pasture. Retired from racing, rodeos, roping and negotiating steep mountains trails, he seemed perfectly willing to play the old man. Fond memories soothed my feelings of loss. We had had a bond. "I respect you but I will get you if you let me." Arrow sent me a clear massage when we started our relationship. We had an understanding.

Smokey was one of those horses everyone loved. We rescued the old horse when we left Paradise Ranch and brought him with us to California. Smokey was an honorable horse who could be relied upon for anything. Although unspectacular, I felt safe with Smokey and could count on his best no matter what I asked of him.

Along with Smokey, we brought Gray Wolf, an Appaloosa gelding. Wolf never wormed his way into my heart like Smokey, Arrow, Sweet Pea or Buck. Once again I was more smitten by looks rather than common sense when I bought this horse. Wolf sported spectacular leopard spots on his white coat, calling attention to his Nez Perce heritage. Wolf turned out to be another flighty horse. He never calmed down after his colt-hood and remained a rebellious adolescent, easily unnerved and impatient. He loved to run and out-walked any horse. We were forever far, far ahead of the pack because of his speedy walk. I never discouraged him from walking fast since that was about the only thing he did well. Fortunately, there were no dramatic accidents with Wolf. He was a mover and shaker who never grew out of his adolescence.

Aside from my two private horses we hauled from the Rocky Mountains to the West Coast, I continued to live my dream of having my choice of ranch horses in Joe's string at my disposal. San Fernando Rey cattle ranch nestled at the foot of the coastal range just a one-day horseback ride from Santa Barbara, its weathered barn hidden under ancient oaks that once witnessed a gun battle with Joaquin Murietta and General Fremont's weary troops liberating the coast from the Mexican government.

Most of Rancho San Fernando's horses were solid, unspectacular ranch horses. Except for a compact small package of an Arabian gelding named Chapo. The cowboys were anything but enthusiastic about Chapo.

"He's no good," they pronounced. "He's useless. A-rabs don't make cow horses." The cowboys avoided anything that had to do with 'that A-rab'. Their macho talk of course was just a defensive way of protecting their reputation as tough cowboys because Chapo had their number. Chapo was smart enough to engineer his unique position in the cow-horse string. Nobody wanted to ride him, consequently he got to rest, play, sleep, eat and he didn't have to put up with the dumb cowboys who didn't know which end was up. He was after all a descendent of sophisticated royal bloodlines with a superior IQ. Chapo, like Arrow, was definitely smarter than the average cowboy. Sweaty cowboy hats, spurs, ropes and selected cuss words hadn't cramped his spirit.

Early in the morning, with dew still on the corral posts, the cowboys sauntered into the corral to catch their cowpony for the day. They carried a nosebag filled with oats. Chapo saw nothing wrong with getting his share and butting in to steal the morning ration. This started the famous Chapo's reign of terror. One particular lanky cowboy, young and green behind his ears, belted Chapo over the nose with the bag's leather strap. Chapo didn't take kindly to such insults from lower human forms interfering with his narcissistic needs. He promptly pinned his ears back and went after the cowboy with his teeth bared and snapping. The panic stricken cowboy actually heard the teeth clicking together like a pair of pruning shears. Instantly intimidated, Dave bolted for the safety of the fence. Since that morning, Chapo reigned supreme. He figured that all cowboys were wimpy, and continued his ears-back-teeth-bared-snap-snap tactic as a morning ritual. Catching a horse in the corral now became a show of bravery and cunning to avoid Chapo. The cowboys conceded that this little horse meant business when Chapo managed to send cowboy after cowboy to the top rail of the fence. Chapo established a reputation and instilled a certain amount of fear, which of course none of the macho men admitted. The cowboys instead increased their criticisms.

"No good A-rab, damned useless, too crazy to work cattle". That was as good an excuse as they could dig out of their tight little Levi pants pocket. A few brave cowboys tried to ride him on cattle drives and instantly pronounced him as hopeless. Chapo danced, bared his teeth, pinned his ears flat and stomped his feet.

I inherited the useless horse. "Let a girl ride him," the cowboys figured, "he's no good for real work." They all knew that girls were also crazy.

Chapo and I were friends from the first day, perhaps because he smelled no chewing tobacco and heard no cuss words. He never ran me out of the corral when I conspired with him against the cowboys, talked to him, and told him that he was not crazy and a fine horse. He experienced none of the rough stuff he remembered from the cowboys who counterfeited a brave image. Chapo appreciated my simple kindness. He did not understand that machismo was an act of bravado and cowboys were really endowed with kind hearts and a certain sense of insecurity.

When I walked into the corral, Chapo ran up for a petting session. If a male walked into the corral and if Chapo could talk, he would have said, "I'll run you off, buster," or, "don't mess with me." I trained Chapo on the finer points of horsemanship. We worked in the arena, in the field and finally with cattle on the open range. He responded to a light hand and to talking. He'd listen with his ears cocked, and when he felt excited on a cattle drive, he'd calm down by hearing to my litany of nonsense words. He transformed into a fine cow horse and the ranch considered him my horse. Even after proven performances on the range, no one wanted to ride Chapo when they watched our game. The cowboys were not aware that he was a good actor. After tiring hours riding in the back forty, all the horses expected to be tied to the fence, the saddle removed and the feedbag attacked over their muzzles. When we arrived at barn, I turned Chapo around and pretended to head out of the corral. It was a dirty trick of course, but his response was a show worth watching. Chapo pinned his ears flat on his head, and snapped his teeth like a turtle. After a minute of playing the game of being outraged, I allowed him to return to his spot by the fence. He knew the game and nuzzled my arm when I stepped off his back, waiting for his rub down and his reward of grain. The cowboys shook their head. "That A-rab is still crazy," they'd pronounce while spitting a wad of tobacco on the ground.

On a warm afternoon, a typical California winter day, the crew and I rode back to headquarters after driving five hundred young Mexican steers to a remote part of the ranch. One of the cowboys ahead of our little group started to uncoil his rope and allowed it drag through the grass. Suddenly, Chapo snorted and stomped his front feet into the grass. Whomp, his hoofs pounded into the earth, chunks of dirt flying through the dense winter grass. The cowboy's rope snapped tight as Chapo struck the rope repeatedly with his hoofs. Chapo's ears pinned flat on his head and he blew and whistled through his flared nostrils. "I'll be damned," one of the cowboys remarked, "that darned horse thinks the rope's a son-of-a-bitchin' snake." For once, the motley cowboy crew admitted that this was one heck of a smart and brave horse. Other horses would have shied away, but Chapo displayed the fearlessness of a warrior. From then on, I showed off Chapo's snake sense and he earned a reputation as the 'snake killer'.

Chapo won barrel races and ribbons at gymkhanas, and placed in Arabian horse shows. He even earned the respect of the cowboys at Rancho San Fernando Rey, especially after the snake incident, but the cowboys never messed with him and were occasionally still run out of the corral and they still called him 'that A-rab'.

Buck Berry, a gray quarter horse, will forever be Number One in my book of horses. When the Hibernian sage wrote: "There are three things a man never forgets and one is a horse," he must have meant Buck Berry. I called him Buck and on most occasions, Bucky Baby. If I could have only one equine love in my life, he was that love. I bought Buck during a wet Rocky Mountain spring. Mud, snow and slush claimed every pasture and field of the ranch below Pikes Peak and it was still nasty cold. Buck was a two-year-old, barely broke to ride. Large liquid eyes reflected a kind soul, set wide apart on a dished head. When his thick winter coat finally shed, a pale silver coat emerged. His white tail was tinged with silver. Buck, even at the defiant age of two, considered all humans his friends. He never learned to kick, buck, bite or pull on a rope. He was born gentle with not one defiant or mean streak under his black hide. Kids crawled under his belly, my two children as tiny tots rode him without mom holding on, yet he loved working, running, turning, racing, and even jumping. He did not require spurs and whips to accelerate into high gear.

I rode Buck on precarious mountain trails where the skills of a mountain goat came in handy. I never needed to worry about plunging to my death on ribbon wide mountain trails perched along precipitous cliffs dropping to a valley a thousand feet below.

He did have some quirks. Although sure footed, when walking uphill, he tended to rush to get to the top and often tripped and fell uphill, catching himself with his nose to get off his knees. The saving grace was that he never tripped downhill, whether at a dead run, or sitting and sliding on his haunches down precipitous slopes.

Aside from a savvy trail horse negotiating terrain specifically designed by God for mountain goats, Buck was also at home in the rodeo arena, the snooty show ring, and on cattle round ups. He loved roping events and barely contained his eagerness in the roping box or the corral. Since I was not an expert roper by a long stretch, Buck maneuvered me into the right place. He worked independent with just the right burst of speed, or slowed down when necessary to place even a bumbling roper in a good position to throw a loop. He needed no training to pull the rope tight while the roper got off to doctor a steer. He helped me look good in the arena as well as the trail. My minor roping successes were actually due to Buck's talented cooperation.

Buck possessed cow sense and he considered cutting out cattle great fun instead of work. He was not a champion cutting horse, but he always got the job done without any fuss or excessive guidance from his rider.

He loved running and earned ribbons in barrel racing. He required no whips, or extra encouragement. His favorite sport was running the bucking horses off a mountain into the home corrals. At Paradise ranch the bucking horses pastured atop a mountain and were chased to the rodeo grounds each Saturday evening.

The chase off the mountain was as thrilling as experiencing a roller coaster ride, jet fighter flight, and parachute jump all at once. As soon as the bucking horses gathered speed and shifted into overdrive, they charged in a dead heat down the mountain, over rocks, through ditches and dodged trees. To prevent the horses from trying to put one over on us and veering away from the direction of the rodeo arena, riders rode flank and rear. The race could be compared to chasing a runaway fright train. Since the bucking horses were unencumbered by a rider, they showed no qualms negotiating anything at breakneck speed, including cliffs. A trustworthy and sure-footed horse was essential unless the rider wanted to take part in a suicide mission. Buck loved the chase and we never encountered any mishaps.

When I found an English saddle in the hip-roofed Paradise ranch barn, I decided to teach Buck the art of jumping. I knew nothing about jumping or English riding, but when winter set in and life turned a bit boring, the new activity seemed a fine way to add some excitement to everyday riding. Buck was better than I at jumping obstacles, and soon my heart thumped with trepidation by jumping ever-higher obstacles. Buck had no problems and enjoyed the new activity immensely. I had to be the one to learn and gather my nerve for each jumping session.

During rodeos, I earned the rare distinction of being one of very few female pickup riders in the saddle and bareback bronc events. Since my cowboy husband was foreman and managed the rodeo, I earned the plum position of pickup rider. Buck learned in no time how a pickup horse better stay out of the way of flying heels. He learned to charge toward the shoulder of the bucking horse and crowd in close while the bronc rider got off. All this had to happen in the breath of a few seconds with little or no guidance from the rider. The pickup rider is busy grabbing and dallying the hack rein, or pulling the flank strap, or just concentrating not being yanked off the horse by an inexperienced bronc rider grabbing for any human part to vault off his bronc. Buck knew all the right moves to avoid accidents. Buck seemed as addicted to rodeo as I. Sunday became his day to shine and show off.

But wrecks happen even to wonder-horses. Buck fell only once when chasing a bucking horse. He tripped, dumped on the ground nose first during a dead run, but managed to somehow right himself, barely breaking his stride. No time for being scared, just time to hang in and stay with the horse, Buck resumed his chase to catch up with the bronc.

Buck helped me become a pickup rider. Of course, rodeo riders didn't figure on a girl helping them off their bronc. During those few opportune seconds when the bronc rider has a chance to get off, he often hesitated because the rider suddenly realized he had to grab a girl to hoist himself from bronc to the pickup horse. Now and then, a bronc rider needed a little encouragement. "Get the...off," I'd yell. The greenhorn bronc riders were picked up by Joe or another male pickup rider because they were too likely to grab the pickup rider around the shoulder or neck and my hundred pounds was no match for a hundred and seventy pound cowboy with fear in his heart.

Buck lived out his life as an old man on green pastures. He left a special legacy. He won a championship barrel racing buckle and he cared for our crumb-crunchers as they grew up. He worked cattle as well as performing as a trail and pleasure horse and jumped hurdles with the enthusiasm of an English Jumper. He was savvy to human foibles and tolerant with the inexperienced. He loved bossing cattle, with a nip now and then on their behind. He followed me about the barnyard without being led. He chased me when I carried a grain bucket and deliberately ran away from him. He pinned his ears back, but as soon as he caught up, he nuzzled my hand as if to say, "Ok, time to stop playing, let's eat."

The old man died from cancer of the mouth. We put him down to spare him further suffering after painful attempts to chew soft mash. I belief a special place had been reserved for Buck in the big world beyond the Rocky Mountains.

Dogs were almost as important as horses. Before we were 'rich' enough to own horses, we owned dogs. They were of course ranch dogs, the kind of dogs that slept outside, couldn't wait to nip, chase or herd anything on four legs, would rather work than bask in the shade, and feared nothing. Most were a Heinz 57 variety, from one purebred Australian Shepherd to a Mostly-Mutt with diversified racial backgrounds.

Dogs saved time, energy, and sometimes injury. They were expected to run an incensed bull into a pen, catch a wild boar that just as soon kill anything with two or four legs, flush out a covey of quail, protect the chickens from skunks and foxes, protect the pickup from anyone with sticky fingers, provide companionship for the crumb-crunchers as they grew up, and of course herd cattle.

Our first dog did not do any of the above. Joe and I found a pudgy bundle of Boston Terrier near the Targhee ranch in Yellowstone Park. We attempted to find the owner, but when no one claimed the black and white bundle, we brought him home with us to the two-room trailer. Of course, he was of no use except entertainment and companionship.

Later, the big dogs entered our lives. We inherited some because the owner did not want them and that was always chancy since we didn't know why the owner gave a dog away, but our budget did not afford the purchase of a registered cow dog. We dared not look a gift dog in the mouth if we wanted free dogs. Most free dogs seemed like a good deal, and we were lucky enough that most of our freebie dogs were a good deal.

Of course, all dogs we acquired had to be trained. No cowboy is dumb enough to give away a free dog already trained as a cow dog. Training cow dogs is time consuming and takes a bit of knowledge in the field of psychology. Any field of psychology will do. Human, animal, horses are born with the same behavioral attributes. Children have much in common with a horse and dog, and even a spouse can be trained in the same manner as a horse or cow dog. All ranch wives have skills in training their cowboy spouses to keep his muddy boots on the porch, leave his sweaty hat in the laundry room, ride the wife's horse when it gets too ornery, and now and then take a weekend trip that isn't to the rodeo.

Once we acquired and trained a good dog, that dog than trained the new pup. Since I already trained a few previous dogs, several horses and a husband, I volunteered for the job of puppy training.

Coach was a natural. The sight of cattle evoked ancient herding instincts. We called him the Heinz 57 with talent. His ancestry included Australian shepherd, German Shepherd and Doberman. I owned one outstanding horse in my life, and Coach was bar-none the outstanding dog of a lifetime. Children sat on him and pulled his stubby chopped off tail, but Coach tolerated the nonsense. He even tolerated our resident cats. At worst, he grumpily moved off to hide someplace safe from little fingers and annoying kittens. He loved people and lingered around company just in case someone remembered to pet him. He also knew his boundaries. Neighbor's homes and the road past the property were off limits, even when a pretty female cur attempted to entice him to visit. He could not claim any watchdog status because he refused to bite anyone, but no one bothered the pickup anyway because he looked mean and fierce. He did however, chase off uninvited dogs unless legitimate visitors accompanied them and then he used his ignoring behavior. Uninvited dogs learned to hightail it far away and lick their wounds if they did not heed Coach's warning. Coach also loved riding in anything. On the hay wagon he perched on top of bales, he balanced himself on tractors just so he could ride along, and thought he was in heaven when he rode in the back of a pickup.

His real passion belonged to renegade steers and wild boars. Born with an appetite for adventure, nothing could be wild enough for Coach. He matched his cow dog talent with any champion sheep dog and then some because he was adapt in the wildest country where a dog had to work out of sight and sound of his master. Sometimes a mean steer or cow kicked Coach, and then his temper flared and the steer or cow was paid back with additional harassing nips to their heels. He'd yip in pain and immediately charge in for more.

Each morning at Rancho San Fernando Rey, in the untamed coastal mountains, the cowboys gathered at headquarters to eschew (with a good wad of chew) which back forty of the ranch needed ridden that day. Running Mexican and Brangus steers from dense brush, roping and doctoring steers or moving them to different sections of the ranch occupied five days in the week. Coriente steers were shipped to the ranch from deep inside Mexico because they were tough and hardy and could withstand heat, brush and diseases. Wiry and smaller than the average feeder steer, they made up in cost by being cheap to buy and cheap to keep in tough conditions, but they were also wild renegades with feral dispositions. A certain number each year disappeared forever in inaccessible canyons. If Coach could have been the cattle buyer for the ranch, he would have bought the wildest Coriente from Mexico. He loved wild boars for the same reason: The challenge and the matching of wits with death. Coach cared little if a boar outweighed him twice or ten times and his tusks were three or five inches long and sharp as knives. When a boar moved through the brush sounding like a freight train, Coach drooled with anticipation.

"Pig, pig, pig," was the password for hunting pigs. "Ssst, get 'em, get 'em," instantly electrified Coach, his ears perked, sniffing and running as soon as he received permission. Off on his pig hunt, he crashed down vertical slopes, penetrating impenetrable brush, and charged into arroyos and canyons. The word fear seemed foreign.

To his detriment, he figured farm animals were also fair game. After finding dead chickens several days in a row our suspicions wandered toward Coach who hung around the chicken yard more frequent than usual. We were horrified when we finally caught him in the act, with a white hen at his feet. On any ranch, a chicken killer is unacceptable, especially when the chickens belong to the boss. We remembered stories about how dogs stopped killing chickens if hung around the dog's neck, although we didn't know if that was an old farmwife's tale or the honest to god truth. Joe and I loved Coach too much to chain him to his dog-house or give him to someone without chickens.

"What do we have to lose," I said when we considered hanging his latest dead chicken around Coach's neck. He carried the chicken until it smelled more than foul. He crept around the ranch yard, not daring to look at us because by now he had figured out he did something very wrong. Each time Coach was in sight, we scolded him. "Bad dog," we repeated, "shame on you, bad dog."

He crawled off on his belly, dragging the smelly dead chicken. We felt terrible for Coach, but kept our fingers crossed that this little trick worked when we finally untied the dead chicken. After that humiliating experience, Coach made it a point to circumvent the chicken house and pretend they did not exist. Even irk-some clucking hens and our notoriously aggressive rooster who strutted his stuff could not entice Coach.

On cattle drives and pig hunts, we paired Coach with a black Airedale. Black Puppy was another 'freebie' dog from a neighbor cowpoke. As in police work, a good cop needs a trustworthy partner and we planned to use the black pup as Coach's pig and cattle partner. Coach had to teach the pup to work cattle and hunt pigs. He patiently played the role model and parent to Black Puppy, but the pup refuse to learn ranch dog behavior and preferred to learn nothing at all. He warded off all attempts at teaching with growling and snapping at his owners and digging himself into one spot or hiding under vehicles. Of course, in a cowboy family, this doesn't cut the mustard. Obedience in animals is about as important as godliness for a preacher. Come here, stay, and heel commands were halfway learned while I remained on the ground with Black Puppy on his leash, but once the commands were repeated from a horse's back, Black Puppy promptly charged under a car or behind some object and growled. Once he jumped into a handy trash can and when I attempted to retrieve him, he alighted from the trashcan, his teeth bared and growling with the best ferocity he could muster.

I decided the game was over before Black Puppy turned into a dangerous anti-social adult. I uncurled my rope and tied it to Black Puppy's collar to prevent his hiding stunts. After mounting my horse, I dallied the rope to my horn and walked off. Black Puppy dug in his heels. No amount of encouragement could budge him from his little piece of earth. I felt guilty about the next tactic, but it worked within a week. I simply took off on my horse with Black Puppy scooting along; his feet still dug in, the dust flying. When he couldn't dig in anymore, he flopped on his back but found out that didn't help either. Finally, when life got too dirty and uncomfortable for him, he emitted a few howls and followed like a normal dog. Soon he learned how to follow behind the horse since I chose a horse that threatened to kick if he tried to follow too close or pass. After a few rope episodes, Black Puppy's learning curve increased.

Although Black Puppy's beginning was shaky and rough, he transformed into an excellent cow dog and partner for Coach. Old man Coach taught him the rest of the tricks of the trade and from then on, Coach and Black Puppy were an inseparable team. Black Puppy never again growled or snapped at anyone. Our little crumb-crunchers loved him, attempting to ride him as if he was a big black horse. They pulled his fur when it was not shaven for hot summer workdays, and snuggled close to his gray beard when he stretched out after a day's work. We learned to love him along with Coach and accepted him as a family member.

In the summer of seventy-four, Black Puppy lost his partner. Coach was shot in the head and left for dead. We found him after days of relentless searching, with a bullet in his head. Coach had become a victim of revenge from a foreman at a ranch where we were involved with the Caesar Chavez union movement. Coach paid with his life at the hands of an angry man who disrespected man as well as beast. We only hoped somewhere in that person's life that karma will bring justice. We could not understand what kind of human I capable of murdering a trusting animal. Cowboys are not that kind of creature.

Skunk was another unwanted dog who found a home with our family. We acquired the Border Collie as the usual freebie dog. She arrived complete with a love for lurking in the barn. Protecting her ranch turned out to be her main mission in life. That Mr. Shannon owned the ranch made no impression on her. She claimed the barn, the yard and the hen house as her domain to be fiercely defended day and night. Aside from her natural instincts for heeling, Skunk's watchdog talent prevented anyone from leaving the safe confines of their car when they drove into the ranch yard. She had a fine set of white teeth she showed everyone except the family. However, that created a problem. The owner of the ranch also could not get out of his car when he visited his cattle ranch. As far as Skunk was concerned, Mr. Shannon might as well pack up and leave. That sat all wrong with Mr. Shannon. He wanted to inspect his pet projects like the horses, the new heifers or the laying hens without his trouser legs chewed up.

Mr. Shannon let it be known that he did not appreciate being held hostage in his car on his own ranch. He called by telephone since Skunk refused to allow him to get out of his car to tell Joe in person. "That dog you have," he tried to be polite, "won't even let me out of the car. You have to do something about that dog."

Skunk could not care less what Mr. Shannon wanted and continued to play vicious guard dog even after our attempt to befriend her with the owner. The problem finally ended in a showdown where we had to find a new home for Skunk or we had to find a new home for us. Skunk lost. We found a fine home for Skunk way out in the boonies with a cowboy who did not have to worry about bosses coming around and bothering Skunk's personal domain.

However, that still left the attack rooster. Joe and I taught an especially feisty rooster to fight. He took to fighting like a beaver takes to a pond. He learned to stretch out into a racehorse kind of sprint, jabbering in excitable rooster language, "Clackclack, clack, clackclackclackclackclack," attacking whatever moved in the ranch yard or got out of a car. We thought him quite smart and funny until he attacked Mr. Shannon. The boss disagreed and did not like the rooster attacking him anymore than he liked the dog streaking after him with teeth bared. Eventually, the rooster found himself in a soup pot and Mr. Shannon bought a new rooster for his pet chicken-house project.

That was the end of our guard animals except for one cat that fancied herself as a guard-cat. Luckily, the cat did not live on Mr. Shannon's ranch. Before the little cowboys were born, Joe and I adopted a pair of brother and sister Burmese cats. The handsome blue-gray cats were smarter than the average house cat and sister turned out to be too smart for her own furry britches. She turned into a vicious aggressor while her brother Klatz was, well, a lover and not much interested in hunting or fighting. Seems nothing frightened Klatz's sister Pewter, not human or dog. She adopted the house as her castle and allowed no one inside except for the family whom she considered her housekeeper and cook. When an outsider knocked on the door, Pewter placed herself in her attack position in front of the door, her back arched, hair standing on end and emitted growls, hisses and her special caterwaul. Visitors were properly impressed. Pewter of course did not fear dogs. To her, dogs were mere critters that dumb humans allowed to populate the earth. She tolerated Coach and Black Puppy with a kind of truce. "I'll stay out of your way if you stay out of mine".

Most of the time, she managed to out-bluff the unlucky dogs that visited with their owners or strayed onto ranch property. Her reputation as a cat to reckon with grew with one particular incident.

"Watch that cat, she runs off dogs," most dog owners warned each other except for one cowboy who couldn't resist the challenge and brought his big bad German Shepherd. The German Shepherd shared his owner's arrogance about cats. Both dog and cowboy strutted toward the barn where Pewter perched on one of her lookout stations. The dog strutted into the barn as if he owned it, and no one knew exactly what happened, but in no time at all the dog streaked from the barn, howling in a panicked high pitch, with a cat firmly attached to the dog's back. The dog raced for his life out of sight. The cowboy didn't have much to say to anyone including his dog when he came back with his tail between his legs, nervously slinking toward the safety of the pickup. We figured at least one German Shepherd exists that will have a life long phobia of cats.

Brother Klatz was just the opposite of feisty and combative. Klatz's favorite haunt was the house and the couch. He loved visitors who made a fuss about him. He curled up and purred tiny squeaks of delight or tiny squeaks of longing, depending on whether he got attention or wanted attention. Klatz appointed himself as guardian of the first crumb-cruncher. He paced when little Shane slept in his crib and complained to us with squeaky pleas if the baby cried. Klatz sat for hours in front of the crib guarding his little charge. As the crumb-cruncher grew into a toddler, Klatz tolerated hair pulling and when little fingers were a bit too energetic, Klatz retracted his claws and swiped at the busy little hands. Klatz grew up with both crumb-crunchers until they were teenagers. We considered him family. He died in a manger on a cattle ranch in Ventura County after thirteen years of raising two little cowpokes. He had grown senile and incontinent. Shane and Travis prepared a warm bed for him in the manger and fed him during the last days in his nursing home.

Pets, cats, dogs, horses, pet chickens and roosters were as much part of ranch life as death and birth. When one of us felt sad or angry, we could always depend on a horse, dog or cat to comfort and soothe our feelings. The critters were part of the big school under the sky that taught the children about life and death and even sex.

The oldest son learned all-you-ever-wanted-to-know-about-sex from chickens. One of our roosters at Happy Canyon Ranch was a sneaky fellow, he learned to hide around the corner of the barn and wait for unsuspecting hens to cluck and peck their way into his proximity. Mr. Rooster then raced from his hiding place and quickly impregnated the indignant hen along with enraged clucking, wings flapping and flying feathers. After one particular time Shane raced to the house and announced with the certainty of a seven-year-old, "The rooster is making love again."

Mom and pop never had to explain the facts of life. They were everywhere, around the corner of the barn, in the corral, the pastures and the hills. The creatures and critters were the teachers and much more. They were as much part of our existence as the big sky, the sun, the rain and the land.

4

All that Cowboyin'

Marrying a cowboy is not a dull proposition. Heck no! The challenges keep the wife either on her toes or down in the dirt and dust. A cowboy's wife has to be creative. Not with art, but with budgets. She has to be brave because her cowboy is facing the chance of injury on a daily basis. She best not think about how he might have been hurt when he recalls this or that wreck that made him the hero for the day.

"Damn, that was somethin' when my rope got tangled up with old Smoky and that bull." She then pictures her one and only caught between a thousand-pound raging bull and a fourteen hundred-pound horse, his life in danger inside the dust cloud kicked up by both beasts.

She has to be adventurous, because she is often in the midst of all that cowboyin'. Staying home with a clean apron and bread in the oven is not an option. She's expected to ride the range, get dirty, hurt, wet and tired just like him. The ranch bosses expect the wife to pitch in, usually gratis.

Yet sometimes, life is monotonous. There are no cities sparkling with entertainment. The big screen is twenty or a hundred miles from home. The communities nearby are one to five blocks of shopping with the most exciting establishment the feed store and the best deal is the five dollars off a pair of Levi's at the Tack and Western store. Sometimes excitement can be had at the post office. The heartbeat of a cow town is the post office and the postmaster or mistress is the best source of gossip.

If the wife spends an hour in town, that means she exhausted all of Main street, from one end to the last business at the other end which is most likely the weigh station or taxidermy. By the time she spends her money of which there is never enough, no further opportunities exist for excitement except for diversions created home on the range.

The local bar is one other option for entertainment and source of important neighborhood information. Sometimes the bar can get mighty exciting. Especially when it's past ten or eleven and too many cowboys warmed the bar stools for too many hours. Add a few motorcycle jocks or other non-cowboy characters who likewise warmed the barstools and exercised their elbows, and you might hear a few comments that rub a cowpoke the wrong way. There is a very good reason why the Maverick in Santa Ynez still has swinging doors. There is also a good reason why the wooden bar stools were exchanged with iron tractor barstools.

Joe and neighboring cowpokes and wives were having a mighty good time one night at the Stage Coach Stop above Santa Ynez, another territorial hang out for cowboys. It was close to the witching hour when a motorcycle dude said something. Then a cowboy said something else. Before we knew it, the bar room livened up with punches, flying bottles and tipped over tables. We girls escaped from the back of the room past the mess and out the front door. Some of the motorcycle dudes looked pretty mean with their brass knuckles. While the fight continued with accelerated action, our cowboy husbands decided they didn't care to talk to the sheriff who would surely arrive any moment from the look of the bartender holding the telephone. A whole passel of battered pickups disappeared down the road toward the old homesteads. Luckily, most nights at the bar were peaceful as long as cowboys terminated their beer-drinking marathon before midnight. Dancing helped because that kept them moving instead of ruminating.

Cowboys take infinite pride in taking no guff from anybody, and Joe was no different. He rarely had to fight, most likely because of his bulging arm muscles from his boxing days and his mean black hat. Aside from ducking a fight and drinking a few beers, dancing the two-step or western swing was about the most exciting entertainment on a Saturday night.

Much of the real entertainment is not found in a bar or on Main Street. The range is where cowboys create their own thrills and melodramas. Sometimes the excitement creates itself, without anybody wanting it.

Many of our adventures in the wild were conceived and carried out because of necessity. Making a living and food in the freezer called for certain adventures. Free food on the table tempted and inspired Joe to indulge in the black art of poaching. The only price of venison steaks, elk roasts or a stuffed goose was the price of one or two bullets. The price of this free food could have turned into several thousand dollars if caught by the game warden.

Most poaching activities were the result of a move to a new ranch when we had not yet shared in a side of beef and the thousand-mile move decimated our checkbook. Since a savings—account is a scarce luxury or something other people brag about, any illegal activity that improved the larder was justified. One such justification arose after uprooting to the great Plain's community of Sedgewick.

Sedgewick is where the Colorado plains wind howls 365 days a year with obstinate determination. There are no quiet days. The wind sounds as if a train is passing through and never stops passing through. Thunderstorms strike with fierce veracity and knock out power to the well, the washing machine and the television. Seems the only creatures that tolerate thunderstorms and the incessant winds are geese. Fields of grain and reservoirs are the ideal feeding grounds for geese. Fat, plump, luscious Canada geese. Fat geese were too much of a temptation for a poor cowboy to deny himself taking up arms and stuff a few in the empty freezer. Their daily honking awakened an ancient longing to hunt, but also visions of Duck le Orange or roast goose stuffed with apples. I am certain that no self-respecting cowboy would show any different inclinations when he lifted his eyes to the heavens to check out the honking and squawking.

"I could get us a couple of those honker's" Joe stated one afternoon as the call of the wild geese in V formations brought the pale blue winter sky alive. They were on their way to feed at the nearby reservoir.

I threw Joe a doubtful look. "Yea, and then you get caught by the game warden. I don't want a thousand dollar goose and you in jail." Joe dismissed my fretting. "I know his schedule, I got it figured out. That man's predictable. I got to get me those geese."

Another V formation passed overhead, their honking drifting in the wind above the prairie. My own thoughts of a plump goose on the table overpowered my anxiety about a thousand dollar goose and Joe eating his meals in jail for a few days and giving his rifles and shotguns as a present to the judge.

On a cloudy late November afternoon, Joe arrived at the house, breathless, locking the door and holding up two plump Canada geese. Duck le Orange had become a reality. As soon as I locked the door, drew the drapes shut, turned out the lights to pretend we were not home, Joe's job was finished and mine started. Without a huge pot for boiling water, the bathtub appeared to be the best solution for immersing the honkers to pluck them nice and clean. With the water heater working overtime, the geese were immersed up to their necks and the plucking proceeded on schedule. They plucked as clean as a baby's behind. I hid the wet feathers in a paper bag and dressed the geese at night in the kitchen with the curtains drawn and the doors locked with a certain amount of paranoia about the boss or the game warden paying us a visit. Not to worry, all went well, the geese were tucked away in the freezer for Thanksgiving and Christmas and the bathtub again became a bathtub instead of a goose-plucking tub. Cleaning the bathtub was the last chore.

I had not guessed how quickly goose feathers dry and then fly away to unsuspecting places all over the house. Although I managed to chase and scoop most of the feathers in the bathroom, I also ended up picking them off the ceiling in the next room, the hall and the walls as far away as the living room.

For the next week, now and then I discovered another tell tale feather. We continued our paranoid state about someone coming to the house.

"Golly, looks like you got yourselves feathers flyin' around," I could already hear the comment.

"Oh, the feather bed busted," I planned to answer. If someone visited, I hoped they were gullible. We met the other cowpoke at the feedlot and the boss at our front door, pretending we were leaving the house. Lucky for us no one visited for a week or two and eventually all of the feathers were apprehended. At Thanksgiving, we praised the goose poaching adventure as well worth the effort. However, we avoided inviting anyone because of the buckshot distributed throughout the goose like tiny secret surprises.

Not all hunting turned into poaching. Most hunting was legal with opportunities that any hunter would die for. A covey of quail, at least fifty to a pail; wild turkey at dusk, wild boars with pork chops the size of a dinner plate, deer that are called venison in fancy restaurants, elk that overstuffed our freezer, and ducks too easy to pick off a pond to brag about. Wild boars were our favorite meat, not just to eat, but to hunt. Wild boar roast, chops and sausage filled much of our freezer in California.

Every cowboy's wife owns a freezer. It is one of those necessary investments, more important than a couch or a dining room table. After all, you can sit down to eat anywhere, but you have to have something to eat. The freezer had to be a large one, freezing at least five hundred pounds of carefully stacked meat packages. Every half year or with a cheap employer once a year, a side of beef was part of the pay for a hired ranch hand. In addition of beef, the freezer also stored locally acquired delicacies. Aside from the prized wild boar, there were deer roasts, deer sausage, deer hamburger and deer steaks. Although city folk considered deer an expensive cut called venison in fancy city restaurants, we called deer the cheap stand by, the meat you eat just so you can stretch the prime cuts of beef and provide a change for the tenderloin of wild pork. In high country, we preferred elk to the less juicy and tasty deer. Elk meat filled the freezer faster then any other game. An elk was considered a year's meat supply, but as with most game, a hunting buddy or a hungry ranch family always shared the meat.

Whenever deer meat graced the nightly fare, comments ranged from "Deer meat again?" to "It's not bad with all the gravy." Contrary to deer, we never tired of wild boar. A succulent roast, pork chops and spicy wild boar sausage was especially popular with company from the city.

Aside from eating boar, California coastal cowboys considered boar hunting a favorite activity. Rolling hills rich with oat grass and mean scratchy underbrush provided a heaven for wild pigs. Russian and Razorback pigs were exceedingly clever and could out-think a dumb human. Boars were temperamental and just plain cantankerous. Their temper compared to that of a drunken cowboy who had just been called a sissy by a Hell's Angel. The boar's intelligence and mean temper presented a challenge that every hunter liked to brag about. On the less than brave side, we hunted pigs with dogs. To hunt pigs without dogs in Southern California's coastal range would have meant crawling on your belly in underbrush, up and down wild and steep terrain, hoping a four hundred pound boar wouldn't decide that you needed to be taught a lesson. Pig dogs could easily put a man's courage to shame. We relied on our brave dogs. The pig dogs thought they'd gone to heaven when they were allowed to hunt their favorite prey. Hunting pigs was far preferable to heeling stupid cattle. Wild boars were even more lucrative to the dogs when Happy Canyon Ranch decided to experiment with a herd of Holsteins. For the dogs, the difference between hunting boars and herding Holsteins was like working as a clerk, pushing pencils and paper instead of flying a helicopter in Vietnam.

To reduce the chance of injury or death, dogs worked in pairs. One dog grabbed one ear and the other dog grabbed the other ear, protecting each other from the boar's knife-like tusks.

Wild boars are as dangerous and ill tempered as a rhinoceros; a trait Coach experienced the hard way on one fateful hunting excursion. The hunt had not been a planned one and Coach did not have Black Puppy by his side, but the sudden crashing in the underbrush that belied the presence of a boar tempted Coach to pursue the wild beast. Coach grabbed the ear of the boar. Unfortunately, Coach did not distinguish between a hundred and 150 pound boar and a 400-pound boar. This one tipped the scales with 400 massive pounds, egotistical as all get out, with many years of fighting under his armor plate. The boar tossed his head to get rid of the attacker, but Coach's instinct to fight to the death this time worked against him. Barking and grunting in rage, the boar flung his head and managed to gouge a tusk into the Coach's neck, ripping his throat. Coach finally loosened his grip on the boar's ear and Joe was able to deliver the fatal shot. Coach bled profusely and appeared to be in the last stages of life as Joe carried him home on his horse to patch up his throat. We did not expect our brave dog to live.

For days, Coach languished in one spot without moving. We nursed him with water and fluids, but Coach did not respond. He could not respond even with a weak tail wag when we attempted to peak his interest with a pig call: "Pig, pig, pig." Limp, never moving his head, he gave little indication of improving. A week later, Coach stirred, and a few days thereafter, his ears perked up when he heard the word pig. He survived the attack and soon drooled at the thought of hunting again.

Months later, when Coach killed a wild sheep he had been sent to flush out and hold down, he experienced post traumatic stress syndrome when he viscously attacked and killed the sheep. We forgave Coach for his trespass because of his traumatic past.

Wild boars were not only dangerous to dogs, but also to humans and horses. Old boars were downright rank. They backed off from nothing, not horse nor cowboy with big hat and gun. Their violent aggression and lack of fear created rather interesting hunting. One morning Joe decided we should test our courage and hunt on foot, without our pig dogs, Coach and Black Puppy. Just before dawn when pigs still harvested fields for grain and acorns, the adventure felt like going to war and not knowing around which bend we would meet the enemy. I preferred to avoid testing my courage with anything larger than a Chihuahua. Fortunately, that morning remained silent and uneventful without a glimpse of a single boar or sow in the early morning fog. I refrained from admitting that I felt relieved. Disappointed, Joe said he intended to use the horse and dogs next time.

One balmy spring evenings when chirping crickets sang their mating songs, Joe received an SOS to help hunt down a wild boar. A poacher shot and wounded a granddaddy boar along the road. The boar was on the rampage to kill or destroy anything it its path. The enraged boar had already attacked a horse, a cow, and mowed down several small barnyard creatures. Joe and other cowboys from Rancho San Fernando Rey seized the opportunity, saddled up and with the dogs in tow, rode into the night to end the pig's rampage and misery. The cowboys found the boar and as expected, the boar charged the horses before the boar's life was brought to an end. The pain and injuries from the poacher's bullet had driven the boar into a frenzy of blind rages and ranchers were afraid for a child closing the barn door or the wife checking on a horse. The boar attack provided all sorts of tall tales and embroidered conversation fodder for the next year.

The cowboys shared the meat from the boar with several ranch families because country folk do not believe in wasting any edible portion of an animal.

We were used to these unexpected gifts for the freezer and larder and always stocked up on butcher paper and kept sharp knives handy.

We also experienced the other side of the wild pig's personality. The gentler, comical side that is usually not observed when boars are hunted. Joe surprised me with a tiny piglet. The plump baby piglet squealed lustily when Joe held it upside down as he recalled another tall cowboy story. "We caught that little tyke right after roping and doctoring cattle past Mt. Baldy. Here we were on foot when he ran right under my legs…"

As usual I believed half the story. The little squirt just happened to be in the way and seemed to have lost his mamma. The cowboys thought it a fine idea to bring the piglet home. We were of course aware that the little squirt would grow into a hefty wild boar, but for the time being we thought it fun to keep the little piggy as a pet. We figured that the new tenant would welcome a fine home in a long neglected and spacious wire pen. Little piggy seemed happy to get his four legs on the ground, but I think he missed his Mama. He ran from one end of the pen to the other, squealing and searching for her. After a few days little piggy calmed down and accepted us as his family. He filled out in all the right places and visitors pointed out that he'd make a good side of bacon in another few months. "Lookie at that hog. You'll have yourself a fine side of bacon."

We called him Here-Pig and Here-Pig soon learned to like people. He had learned when a two-legged creature approached the pen he might get his hide sprayed with water. As soon as he spotted one of us, he snorted and run back and forth by the fence, as if calling out "come on now, I'm hot, bring the hose." He delighted in a shower from the hose, snorting and rolling in ecstasy and rooting himself into bliss. In time, Here-Pig grew too huge to be contained by a woven wire fence and he did indeed end up as bacon and pork chops. We did have a bad conscience whenever he graced the breakfast and dinner table.

The abundance of wild pigs in southern California brought them into many parts of everyday life. They were hunted, tucked into freezers, eaten with gusto at breakfast and dinner, but provided the stuff for telling tall tales and hero stories. They also rooted up fields, scared hunters with their cunning and intelligent nature by doubling back and hunting the hunter. They helped themselves to their share of feed spread out for the ranch horses and cattle in corrals and home pastures. The pigs knew how to scout free food and were not shy about helping themselves.

On one of those lazy mild spring evenings, we decided to observe their nightly pilgrimage to the free food supply in the horse pasture. For safety's sake, we climbed a large sturdy oak in the pasture. Soon, we heard the rumble of running hoofs and the anticipation snorted by plump boars and sows. In awe, we observed the mass of black boars in the lead, followed by no less than two hundred sows, stringy tails pointing straight up with excitement. The weaners, squealing in protests and fear that the adults would leave them behind, brought up the rear. Barbwire fences never deterred any decent pig. They dug a path under the first strand and scooted through as if the hole had been greased. They charged with grunts of delight as they reached the piles of hay spread apart for the horse's nightly ration. The horses ignored the grunting guests. Some never looked up, used to the nightly thievery and the smells of pig. The air permeated with the odor of musk, hay and fresh mud.

We counted the chunky black razorback boars, bristles as wiry as a barbecue brush on their humps, and the black pigs sporting white blotches because of interbreeding with tame pigs from Spanish missions over a hundred years ago. A few old granddaddies moved an impressive bulk with ivory tusks curved outward from their black snouts. We counted an army of no less than 250 and remained imprisoned in our tree until they sauntered off to another part of the pasture, rooting through new batches of feed.

Most ranches, because of the pig's prolific existence and rooting up fields, stealing feed and nasty temper, allowed controlled hunting to restrain their numbers. However, one neighbor thought it his duty to preserve the pigs, no matter what the numbers. The foreman at the Janeway ranch, part of a stately Spanish land grant, distributed feed specifically for pigs. He did not bother spreading his welfare feed beyond the ranch buildings, but dropped generous portions throughout the ranch yard. Visiting always turned into a touchy situation. A visitor who wasn't overly brave didn't simply walk up to the ranch house, but called for assistance to pass the rooting and snorting pigs eyeing the human intruder. The pigs nonchalantly sauntered between the car and the ranch house. They were everywhere except inside the house. The pig trapped all but the bravest visitor in the car. During one of my visits, usually accompanied by apprehension, I hesitated to walk back to my car, since I had to pass a monstrous boar decked out with a set of impressive yellowing tusks. "Go on," the foreman said, not concerned, "don't you worry none, Blaster here will keep ya safe."

I eyed the little dog that was about the size of a dime compared to the pig, but I how could I let the foreman know I was a complete wimp? Poised for a sprint with one eye on the boar and the other on the car door, I walked to my vehicle. The dog trotted toward my car without looking at the boar. Perhaps his job was not much different than that of a rodeo clown who needs to run interference between the bull and the rider. The boar apparently knew the game and did not challenge my progress to the car.

The best boar story, according to local cowboy lore, happened quite by accident. Macho city hunters, who ignored keep-out-violators-will-be-prosecuted signs, often poached boars on ranches. On moonlit nights, a mysterious poacher had been killing off boars by the dozens, leaving the carcass to rot and taking only their heads. Trophy hunting was as taboo among cowboys as the devil is to the Catholic Church. The cowboys ended up obsessing about catching the poacher. "I'm gonna nail 'em. Just let 'em make one mistake. Damn, I'd like to catch that rotten S.O.B." Their comments indicated increasing restlessness.

The cowboys at Rancho Santa Fernando Rey champed at the bit to catch the culprit. Joe and the other cowpokes were finally presented with an opportunity to end this poacher's career when they discovered a strange vehicle driving late at night past corrals and cattle pens at the headquarters of the ranch. Since this was the only vehicle access to the ranch without a locked gate, the cowboys figured the stranger had to return on the same road. They rolled their sleeping bags, collected ammunition for their best firearms, brought a few cold ones, and waited out the night by the barn overlooking the ranch access. In the wee hours of morning, the strange car returned. The cowboys promptly yelled. "Stop, get out 'a the car!"

They received an answer from a bullet zinging toward the voice in the night. The answer was the wrong one with trigger-happy cowboys. The cowboys found an opportunity to play Wild-West shoot-out. Zing, zing! Shots rang back, hitting bushes, rocks and dirt. The bullet exchange continued back and forth for a while, the stranger hiding in the bushes. A well-placed shot into a tire ended any chance of lighting out of there with the car and the culprit finally gave up. Turned out he was indeed the midnight poacher, caught hot-handed after dozens of moonlight raids.

The cowboys of Rancho San Fernando Rey were in a story telling mode for the next year and probably are still telling their pig poacher stories to their grandkids.

"Yup, I remember when some son-of-a-bitch butchered one hog after another, but he wasn't smart enough, not on that one night. Here we were, I got my twenty gage, had me my .44 magnum too…"

Boar stories were more plentiful in Southern California simply because that's where the big boars roamed. Mountain lion stories followed as the number two wild tales only because there were fewer chances for encounters than with boars. At San Fernando Rey Ranch, because of its immense expanse of mountain terrain jealously guarded as a game preserve, cowboys had a chance to add a lion story to their repertoire of wild experiences. A game warden controlled the hunting to assure ample proliferation of wild game. Cowboys could hunt to their heart's content without making a dent in the game population. Lion encounters were considered the crème de la crème. Every cowboy hoped to claim at least one brave lion encounter. The lion stories included roping a lion although no one so far had proven a real lion roping adventure. For once, the roping story turned out to be true and the cowboys could prove their adventure. Joe and Buddy made sure no one could call them a liar by bringing the lion home. Come hell or high water, they were going to transport the lion to the ranch with his legs tied to a pole.

The story went like this: "We spotted this here young lion stalking after prey, didn't see what he was stalking, but he looked like he was real tired. He must've run a long ways and never caught what he was runnin' after. Maybe a deer or rabbit. We got real interested beings the lion didn't pay much attention to us, and we followed him for a ways. Maybe he'd been hungry for a long time and was still interested in gettin' whatever he was after. Anyways, we had to start runnin' the horses to keep up with him, and the more we ran after him, the more we thought how easy it would be to rope the little shit. He was already tired and probably couldn't run of from us. I shook out my rope and looked over at Buddy. He grinned and shook out his rope. The trick was, we knowed that if one of us caught his head, the other better catch the heels real fast, or we might have a lion jump into our laps. We decided to chase him to get him even more tired. The horses didn't like it but they went along. We figured the more winded he was the less fight he'd have in him. We finally roped the critter and Buddy was lucky, or maybe it was me that was lucky. Buddy was set up good to get the rope on his head. So we stretched him out real tight and the lion fights, but not real bad. Now comes the hard part; figurin' how to get him back home and how to get the rope off his head and tie his heels. We knew that if we told anybody we roped a lion without the evidence, they'd laugh us outa the country. We spotted a good strong branch and while our horses kept the ropes tight 'cause they were good and scared. We got off and tied his hind feet to his front feet and then tied him to the branch. The lion was so tired by now that he didn't put up much of a fight. We got the rope off his head, which I think was tremendously appreciated by the horses. They had been awfully nervous, but tried to keep their cool. We were able to carry him back in the two-ton truck that we used that day to haul horses behind Mount Baldy. Course, we had to come back for the horses after we drove the truck home with the lion inside. They would of never gone up that ramp anyway with the lion in the back that they thought they just got rid of."

So the story went, and we had to believe it because the lion had been let loose in a fully enclosed pen behind our house. The cage was large enough for the lion to jump around a bit, but he sulked and with fear and suspicion, lay in one place. We immediately found a deer to butcher, but for two days, he remained in one corner, refusing to eat. He was a beautiful young lion, the color of tarnished gold, not quite grown into an adult, probably a teenager just learning to hunt on his own. After two days, his courage returned. "Chhh, chhh," he hissed, growled, and devoured the chunks of deer meat. We were left with a lion we had no clue what to do with, the part that Joe and Buddy forgot to think about. The boys insisted that if we turned the lion loose on the ranch, he might figure this home and he'd return to find those good chunks of free deer meat. "He might chow down on the dogs," Buddy insisted. We called the local zoo and to our surprise, they wanted the lion. Few visitors at the Santa Barbara Zoo know that the lion was there because two cowboys wanted to make a tall lion story come true.

The lion placement was not for money, although we were always in sore need of an extra buck. The opportunity to earn an extra fifty or a hundred dollars presented itself when one of the owners of Rancho Sam Fernando lost prize sheep of some unusual breed and worth more than everyday sheep. The owner of the ranch had earned a reputation as a cheapskate and the sheep were most likely worth hundreds of dollars, even a thousand a piece, but he placed a fifty-dollar bounty on each sheep's head. He asked Joe would he be interested in spending his day off to find these exotic sheep. We immediately multiplied fifty by five and although that seemed an underpayment, we would do almost anything for a couple of hundred bucks.

This affair, we figured, should be just like hunting wild pigs, except the sheep had to be brought in alive. The owner fussed some more, and wanted us to understand clearly about the sheep's value. "Remember, those sheep are unusual, very expensive. I've got to have them in good shape".

"Gotcha," Joe reassured the fussy owner, "we'll treat those little fellas with kid gloves."

"Uhu," I thought to myself, "since when does Joe like sheep enough to call them little fellas?"

The terrain the sheep used as their escape hideaway did pose a minor problem. This was the ferocious side of the ranch, the precipitous slopes of the coastal range, where underbrush walled off access to anyplace, where boulders the size of suitcases tumbled down sheer rocky inclines. A good place for wild pigs and sheep, but not for humans and horses.

We saddled up on a hot July morning, picking the best of our two pig dogs, Coach and Black Puppy and of course chose the best of our mountain horses. After the horses were trucked to the bottom of the mountain, we chose a fire road as access to the bowels of the mountain. Wild vegetation, thorny impenetrable underbrush where only snakes, tough skinned pigs and sheep could penetrate covered the entire mountain. Cliffs forbade access in places where brush grew sparse. We hoped the dogs would smell the sheep and flush them out for us, maybe hang on to their sheep ears until we tied a rope around each one. The day was full of promise and anticipation. It all seemed quite simple.

Phenomenal luck was with us soon after ascending the mountain. One of the exotic sheep stood right in the middle of the road, just like a statue, and I simply threw a rope over the sheep's head, but before I tightened the noose, the sheep wiggled out of the loop. The prize sheep sprinted around the other side of a large boulder in the middle of the road and disappeared down a ferocious incline.

"Too bad," I said, feeling guilty I had not pulled the rope fast enough.

"No big deal," Joe answered, "lets just send Black Puppy and Coach down the hill." We were not discouraged and still planned on earning at least 200 dollars. If we found one sheep that easy, we should be able to find the other sheep. We fig-ured sheep stay close together. Where there is one, there are four or five," I said.

We simply hatched plan two, waiting for the dogs to do our dirty work. The dogs were more than ready to chase anything on four legs, their tongues hanging out, and beady eyes searching for the wave of a hand and a "Go get 'em."

Coach and Black Puppy surely thought this was one more pig hunt. They crashed, fell, slid and tumbled down the incline. At the bottom of the ravine, the dogs barked and yelped to announce a sheep in captivity. Joe pointed down the slope. "Let's go get em'. You coming?"

I peeked over the edge, and although not a sissy in rough country, I decided this descent should be left to mountain goats, not horses. "Down there' was not where I wanted to ride. I answered, "No thanks, you can have all the fun. I'll watch and wait on top."

"You sure?" Joe asked again.

"See ya!" I said as he urged his horse over the cliff.

Joe's horse managed to crash and bounce down the incline, rocks rolling, slid-ing and cracking against boulders. At the bottom, Joe discovered the descent had been for naught. He yelled up the bad news. "Damn, one of them sheep is dead. Coach got him. Looks like a mess."

We speculated that Coach experienced flashbacks from his prior pig attack and decided to chew up his bounty instead of waiting for fangs to slice his throat.

To coach, sheep were nothing more than wild boar with a wooly coat. To our disappointment, not just one, but two sheep were dead, and the others evaporated into the jaws of the mountain. "Darned," I muttered to myself. I really wanted that two hundred dollars.

We continued to scout for the rest of the sheep, but never found them again until we finally gave up our pursuit and sweet dreams of extra money. We kept the botched sheep capture a deep dark secret from the ranch owner.

Aside from sheep hunting, pig hunting and searching for renegade steers, there were other opportunities to ride in God's most savage and feral mountains. Riding through the brush and precipitous inclines often seemed impossible and only bravery or sometimes stupidity could get you into, up and over the coastal terrain. Heavy chaps, jackets and your hat pulled down real tight helped ward off everything from branches with ice picks, to lethal stickers, ticks, and poison ivy. Rattle snakes, boars, big cats and ringtail coons called this home. The mountain brush was useless to cattle ranchers and if left undisturbed, swallowed up grazing land like a swift growing cancer growing as fodder for wild fires.

Every few years these happy hunting grounds were scorched to avoid wild fires and provide additional grazing for cattle. For a few years the terrain turned into civilized grazing land until once more, after wet winters, the tangled and impenetrable growth devoured the golden slopes. Controlled burns were no small event, but a multi-ranch and forest department undertaking. One particular year, Rancho San Fernando Rey designated ten thousand acres around Mount Baldy with its wild canyons, arroyos and escarpments as a burn area. I considered a ten thousand-acre fire far too thrilling to stay home to watch the ranch burn from our house. I wanted badly to be part of this adventure.

The fire crew consisted of cowboys packing incendiary sticks specifically designed to torch grass, trees, and brush. Horses were the only transportation into the narrow steep canyons surrounding Mount Baldy. Fire trucks remained stationed on the outlying areas, and roads were used as fire breaks. Someone had to ride way down into canyons and arroyos to start the fires in those untamed, remote places.

The horses didn't exactly enjoy this endeavor, especially when they discovered a bush torched next to them, the tinder-dry branches exploding and licking at the horse's tails. However, it hastened the horse's departure back up the mountain.

We spread out and rode into gullies, dead-end canyons, ravines and arroyos. The only way to ride into those places was to squeeze, jump or bust through shrub to reach the lowest starting point. The idea was to get to the lowest, meanest spot, torch the dry grass and shrub and hope the horse could out-race the flames up the mountain. But not to worry, the horses busted out as fast as they could leap, scramble and bounce up the precipitous terrain when they heard the whoosh from the first torched brush. The land had been parched since the hot, dry summer and within moments the whoosh grew into an explosive inferno. The first burning brush transformed into a wall of flames racing uphill like an angry rhino. Everything alive dashed ahead of the roaring and leaping fire. The horses did not care if their rider stayed on. This was not a time to fall off and even the most egoistic cowboy held on to the saddle horn for dear life. Along with the saddle horn, I grabbed the mane as we leapt up nearly vertical slopes. I let my horse have his head, figuring he could do a better job then I escaping to safety. Along with the horses and riders, everything with legs, wings or scales raced from the flames. Snakes, ground squirrels, deer, pigs, birds, buzzards and other assorted brush dwellers. Cowboys and horses were not concerned about other creatures and the creatures were not concerned about horses and riders. The heat was on, and only escape mattered. For safety's sake, two riders were assigned to each canyon. However, it is doubtful the other cowboy could stop his panicked horse to pick up a fallen rider.

The mountain exploded in a solid wall of flames, the sky turned black and the land changed to orange, yellow and red. Oak trees popped from the heat. Thump, crack, a tree exploded, then whoosh, the tree transformed into a torch, fueling brittle dry grass that devoured more brush land. When it was all over, the brush gone, the ground charred black with glowing embers, the ashes settled on everything, pickups, ranch buildings, trees and fields.

Until the following spring, bleak skeletons of brush and trees stood as witness to a desolate land uninhabitable for cattle and wild life. For a few days following the fire, ashes and hot cinders pulsated on charred brush and grass. Huge, ancient oaks were the only survivors and stood forlorn in the wilderness, but oaks rely on fire to proliferate their specie. The acorns need fire to germinate, and before one could spot the first breath of life on the charred ground, the acorns popped and swelled below ash covered hills. After winter rains, the dead mountain revived. Life burst forth everywhere and the incinerated landscape transformed into a vivacious celebration of youth. Tender, pale green peeked from the ashes and by late spring, Mount Baldy dressed in a new spring gown of emerald green, smooth and groomed with a fresh hair cut.

The day following the fire, a cowboy's young dog strayed onto the seared earth and charred fields still smoldering under the dead ashes. His soles were burned to a crisp and within one painful moment, he became a useless cow dog. The cowboy was interested in serviceable animals and said he could not afford a laid up dog that wouldn't earn his keep. We took in the burned stray and called him Coach. I made little booties for him that he wore on his salved paws. Coach knew instinctively he could not gnaw on his booties and soon got used to walking around awkwardly with homemade dog booties. His burned paws were eventually replaced by pink skin.

The following spring, Coach healed from his ordeal just as the charred landscape healed from its scorched state of dead earth. Coach bloomed. He figured we were not only his saviors, but also his family. His loyalty and his love never faded for one moment while he was alive.

Although controlled fires created a melodramatic day trying to out-race the angry flames; uncontrolled wild fires were the ones cursing the land. One particular wild fire at first appeared harmless with no threat to ranches. Contained on the other side of the Figuarillo mountain ridge, we were sure fire fighters and fire bombers would contain its progress on uninhabited forest regions. But on day three the cursed Santana winds raced from the blistering desert and fanned flames toward the mountain ridge until the fire crowned the edge like the corona of the sun. From the ridge, the flames licked their way toward tinder dry grassland on the lower back forty of Happy Canyon Ranch. The air tinged with gray clouds. An acrid stench of ashes forecast impeding doom. We called them the Santa Ana winds although technically, they were the Santana winds. They fueled flames eating up grassland, brush and oak like an invasion of locusts. There was no time for a roundup. We jumped into the pickup and raced past a wall of fire to ranch gates leading away from the ever-hungry flames, hoping cattle remembered their escape routes. The heat singed grass and trees beyond the orange and red wall, and smoke and ashes swirled in the gray stained sky. The sun set long before official sunset.

When we thought the animals safe, we stepped on the gas toward home. By now only a half a mile of tinder-dry field separated our home from the hungry flames. We led the horses from the ranch corrals into a field on the opposite side of the road. We opened the chicken pen, hoping the hens and roosters could predict the danger before we rushed to pack a few precious belongings. We threw together clothing, photo albums, jewelry, guns and a box of important papers. We packed the kids among our salvaged pile of mementos and rushed to a friend's ranch where we left everything off including the kids to hasten back to the ranch. The flames stubbornly licked and crawled across the meadow gaining a few feet here, were driven back a few feet there as if a football team played toward the goal.

Fire fighters bulldozed the field, hacked the brush, and eyed the house at the end of the field. The flames in the field, just a few hundred yards from the house, were finally starved into submission.

This close call had not been the only one when we packed a pickup and car with possessions, a few clean and warm clothes and of course the guns. In 1969, Southern California drowned in one the worst floods in since white settlement in California. For four days and four nights, rain poured relentlessly on the already saturated earth. Rivers formed where there had been no rivers. Waterfalls raced down mountains through every opportunistic crevice and arroyo. Flat meadows transformed into lakes and reservoirs swelling to dangerous levels and threatened to break the dams. Water rushed and gushed where there had been no water for a hundred years.

When we lived at Rancho San Fernando Rey, homes hid below thousand-year oaks in a narrow valley, choked by brush at the foot of a precipitous mountain. The ranch's four homes were tucked between the mountain side and an abrupt cliff plunging into a river wandering through telltale stretches of boulders and jagged rocks from past floods. During summer months, the scorching California heat dried the river to a trickle except for a few pools under shady trees, prized spots for watering man and beast during searing hot afternoons. Frogs and turtles migrated to the last few shady pools hidden below boulders and bay trees. In winter the river swelled but never enough to prevent horses and pickups from crossing to the other side.

In sixty-nine, when the heavens opened its floodgates, the river swelled and became a crescendo of roaring noises, ripping at the shores until the vicious water gnawed the shore into chunks, snatched for a wild ride downstream. We watched with both fascination and dread. Our ranch homes, a hundred feet up on the cliff seemed safe for now, but headquarter corrals and barns stared the river straight in the eye. Beyond the barns, national forest land claimed the narrow valley with charming log cabins. The homes, built of rough logs and cedar, were now naked on the shore of the river and in mortal danger of being ripped off their foundations. Those nearest the river could count on a swift death. On the third day of the flood, the river claimed its victims. Roofs, refrigerators, cars, trees tossed up and down on angry waves as the current rushed without mercy toward the open stretches of the Santa Ynez valley. Cattle drowned, some trapped on sandbanks, others losing their footing on muddy ground. Water surged from every edifice, arroyo or crack in the earth to join the main tributary. The flood claimed anything in its path and the incessant thunder of the river competed with the continuous drumming of rain of rain.

The cowboys were helpless. The river cut them off from the grazing land. They could only hope that most cattle were not foolish enough to wander toward their death. We too were captives of the high ground with nowhere to escape but toward doc's ranch house, idyllically situated on a bluff high above the ranch homes. We figured doc's house would be our refuge in case Gibraltar dam above our canyon broke. After doc's place, the bridge had already been torn from the road and prevented any further passage to the grocery store and the civilized world. We spent night and days helplessly watching the spectacle and waiting for the rains to end and waters to subside.

Sleeping fitfully on the third night, I woke during the wee hours of the morning to sounds of slap, slap, slap against the wall of the bedroom. When I peeked out the window into the gray morning light to investigate the strange sounds, I discovered a lake outside our bedroom window, right up to the windowsill, glistening in the grayness of early dusk. I figured the glistening lake as a mirage. The river could not have risen a hundred feet above our cliff, I reasoned. Still puzzled, Joe and I threw on warm clothing and rushed to the front door. We woke Buddy to figure out what to do.

"Oh hell, it's just some little ol' stream coming off the mountain," Buddy said in his never-get-excited voice. The problem of course was that our home squatted in its path of a little ol' stream that had turned into a torrent. Buddy and Joe and the other neighbor cowboys grabbed shovels and managed to dig trenches around the sides of the house, coaxing the shored up water to divert around each side. Sleeping afterward was impossible. Our already pitiful sense of safety evaporated with a renewed vigor of the downpour.

On day four, rumors started that the dam at the end of the valley would soon be unable to tolerate the increasing water level. Gibraltar dam perched high up on the mountain, at the end of our narrow dead end valley. If the dam broke, we would be imprisoned in its path with millions of gallons obliterating the ranch.

Rumors were somewhat verified by radio reports. The dam officials did not admit that the dam was in danger, but people were warned to listen to the radio. "No problem," the state damn officials announced, "be prepared, just in case." We heeded the 'just in case' and packed the pickup and car with valuables and clothing, photo albums, jewelry and horse gear. Those were the days without little crumb-crunchers, and our most precious belongings were stowed in the old Studebaker.

We waited. The cowboys and their families in the other three houses waited. We entertained ourselves by observing the river's victims float past, tossed about by the swollen waves. Here was someone's car, a roof from a cabin, a refrigerator, trees, fences and parts of homes. During the day we wandered down to headquarter corrals, marveled at the half-mile wide river licking like a giant tongue at the corrals. The horse pasture closer to the river had been under water for the last two days, and the horses had been moved uphill. They were safe unless the dam broke. The cattle at the other side of the river had to fend for themselves and most of the steers, we hoped were in the backcountry except for those unlucky ones wandering near the river. We could not guess at the number of cattle that might drown. A tally of heads after spring roundup would reveal the losses. Work would begin when the rains ended and the torrential river receded enough to cross over to the fifty thousand acres of ranchland.

On day five, the rains ceased. The dam never broke. We unloaded the pickup, kept the freezer lid shut because of the power outage, and wondered how to buy beer with the bridge washed out. Electricity had been non-existent for the past three days. The utility company counted on two days before they restored electricity, but maybe five or six. In another week, the Gas Company promised to repair the lines. The Seabees promised to install a temporary bridge over the road to the main highway and grocery store.

We could live with candles, bread and jam, but one of the more serious disasters was the depletion of beer. The nearest store with beer and fresh meat sat at the other side of the bridge. Since beer is an important part of cowboy diet, ingenuity from a few desperate cowboys resulted in a footbridge across the roaring tributary that tore out the main road. A few cowboys dared to cross the dead oak tree.

I checked out the angry muddy torrents below and decided that we could wait for beer. Even beer was not worth the precarious crossing. Kind neighbors, who were either braver than we or perhaps dumber, brought us back two six packs of beer. Joe was happy, and we spent days surveying the damage as the muddy waters grudgingly gave back muddy patches of land.

At first, the horses flat out refused to cross the swollen river. They appeared to have much more sense than the cowboys who tried to sweet talk their mounts to cross the river. When the sweet talk had no effect, the cowboys used their spurs and cussed a little. That didn't work either. Some of the horses at first gave in, but leapt back to shore as soon as one hoof found the slippery mud or tearing currents below their bellies. The horses were less than enthusiastic about the chances of drowning and were not concerned about the cowboy's ego to be the first brave one to cross the river.

From day one after the rains ended, an unspoken contest existed about who would cross the river and be the first man on the other side. Finally, one of the cowboys managed to fool his horse into plunging into the current. Promptly they swept downstream but the horse had the good sense to swim and lunge with an eddy of the current toward the far shore. They were safe, although a bit downstream from where they started. Naturally, the other cowboys could hardly decline the challenge. Eventually all the horses gave up fighting and crossed. For the next few days, the horses started to trust the cowboys that they would not drown in the muddy water and plunged into the river without a tantrum, swimming and leaping to the other side. I waited until the waters receded enough that my horse did not mind the swim. I trusted his judgment more than the cowboy's judgment mired in hero pursuit.

Two weeks after the flood, ranch trucks once again drove across the river, loaded with five horses that now rode to the back of the ranch in comfort instead of swimming and plodding along miles of muddy roads.

Within months, the land sucked up the last of the water, roads were patched, and the earth healed itself although scars of new riverbeds left timeless reminders. Cowboy tales about the flood and crossing the big one grew from realistic to the same old fantastic cowboy stories reminiscent of fish stories that grow in proportion.

"Hey, yesterday my horse got caught in all that junk that's still floatin' the river. Could a' drowned."

"Yea? Well I got nearly kicked in the head when the other horse lunged. You know I would have drowned."

Every cowboy recalled his favorite tale. The stories were laced with a hint of truth but did not escape elaboration. The flood of sixty-nine provided for lots of heroism and story telling until the next cataclysmic weather, horse wrecks, cow punching disasters, boar and mountain lion hunt, or shoot out.

5

"Mammas, don't let your Babies Grow up to be Cowboys"

Some would call us vagabonds. Others would call us drifters or unsettled. When Joe and I were first married, we hankered to be free as wild geese, free to move from ranch to ranch, to explore, experience new pastures, and always, hopefully, greener grass. The grass wasn't always greener. It often yellowed and dried, with cactus and rocks. The same time one of my gardens bloomed yellow and red with fragrant roses, the resplendent yet treacherous locoweed sprouted in sparse pastures to poison horses and livestock.

When we were first married, our possessions were portable ones, and we could pull up stakes on a moment's notice. We owned little more than a teepee full of personal things and a few pots and pans. Children did not fit into our lifestyle. They needed roots, a school, steady friends and steady parents. We were unable and resistant to seek permanence and security and we longed for adventure and the unknown. Kids would slow us down. We put off the kids for seven years.

But father time knocked on our door. Joe's hairline receded and I pushed thirty. If we wanted kids we needed to figure this out real soon. We concluded we indeed would enrichen our life with a couple of kids and we figured that somehow we could become stable enough to raise them. Knowing only a vagabond life with no idea how normal stable families survive, we counted on a miracle to change our nomadic lifestyle. Perhaps, I secretly hoped, kids would force us to settle down.

The thought that kids might enrich our life originated in the high Colorado Rockies near Grand Lake, in a tiny log cabin where a wife has plenty of time to contemplate the future. Joe worked at odd jobs on road crews in between ranch jobs. The job was one of a dozen when a cowpoke is out of a real cowboy job and perhaps Joe had too much time to think melancholy thoughts. "My brother's boys will never become cowboys," Joe reasoned, "we need a cowboy to carry on the tradition."

We watched the six children belonging to the rancher next door. "Not six," I said, "but two might be nice."

Winter was on its way and there were no jobs with the road building gang when snow blanketed the mountain world. It was time to move and search for something resembling a home to raise children. Sometimes I worried about our new quest that would end in taking on a whole lot more responsibility than the past seven married years.

"You have to get a job where we can stay," I urged my husband. We need an extra bedroom. We just got to find a good place." Eight months remained to accomplish my dream of a steady job."

"Don't worry, little bride. Something will come along in the Western Live-stock Journal. Mark my word," Joe said with more confidence than he should have had.

I wanted to believe. So I did.

We moved out of the high mountains on an icy cold day to the blustery Colorado plains. The promise of spring was in the air, the promise of a place to raise young'ns. A spacious ranch house should satisfy our needs, we hoped. The ranch house was as promised and designed for children; a place for a child to run and play on a sunny porch or hide in the half-finished basement and slumber in a bedroom with dormer windows. The mowed green yard was fenced, with lovely shade trees and flowers peeking along the fringe of the fence. We didn't have enough furniture to fill eleven rooms, but we did fill our freezer with prime cuts of beef from the feedlot. "If you want", the boss said, "you can keep a cow."

We found a doctor in a dusty Nebraska town on the Colorado border and figured we'd settle down for a spell. The foreman's job never materialized, and Joe was soon dissatisfied and grumpy from too much work on foot in muddy cattle pens.

The radiance of my pregnant state could not be diminished by the constant winds or Joe's complaints of, "What do I need cowboy boots for anymore?" or, "What do they think a horse is for?" Armies of obese flies did not discourage my glowing state of being and heavy manure-molasses smells could not discourage my pregnant world. I of course recognized the handwriting on the wall. We would move.

At first, we were clueless on how to escape the fly infested feed lot. The more pregnant I grew, the more hopeful I found my state of life, believing in one more miracle. The new life I now felt kicking and squirming demanded more attention than our restless and dissatisfied plight. Joe was grumpy and less hopeful, less intent on reveling in my new state of body and mind. His muddy overshoes and his unused saddle were reminders that this was not our heaven.

"Those damn farmers", he griped, "don't they know what horses are for. The next job, by god, I'm gonna ride again. Wait and see, we'll get something before that little tyke gets here."

I believed and busied myself with preparation for the new tyke.

This was farm country, home to farm folks who worked from sunup to sundown with no reserve energy left for fun activities. On the feedlot, few activities consumed my time except sewing baby blankets and a christening dress. Some days I rode the prairie to explore the Overland Trail where wagon ruts were silent witnesses to pioneer days. It was a lonely, windswept place, the immensity of the land and the sky dwarfed all human thought and left me dreaming of the excitement of a new life. The prairie grass bent under the force of the wind and filled the uninhabited spaces with its constant whine. It was a good place to dream and a good place to gain strength. If those pioneers could triumph over their hardships, so could we.

When we sorted cattle, despite the owner griping that a man ought to be on foot, I rode my horse in the alleys and pens and I told no one I was pregnant since the boss might have become nervous and forbid me to ride the pens. As far as I was concerned, riding a horse was not much different from heavy housework. I knew most men would not understand.

The event would not have been as embarrassing had there been no audience. That day we were separating cattle for a prospective buyer who brought his entourage. Along with our boss, the foreman and a few friends and neighbors, I provided the entertainment that day. Joe and I alternated cutting out steers the buyer selected and running them away from the bunched up herd to a loading chute. One particular selected steer attempted to bolt back to the bunched up herd, and my proficient horse, quick as a cat, bolted in the steer's path to cut him off. I continued in a straight line while Wolf did his duty as a cutting horse. I sailed to the ground, hit the wooden rail with my neck on the way down and sprawled in the middle of the narrow alley. The steers quickly assessed the situation, bolting and charging en masse down the alley. They shifted into high gear toward my prone body. Lying helplessly on the ground, they looked much larger than the sorry little critters from a horse's back. I attempted to move, but my legs and arms refused to cooperate. This was it, I thought, I will be trampled and my unborn cowboy will not survive this show. The farmers who usually moved at snail's pace were suddenly quick footed and one of them jumped in front of my body, waving his arms to head off the determined herd. Confused and frightened, the bunched up herd decided that it was not a good idea to continue the flight down the alley. By this time feelings returned to my arms and legs and with the help of the fence, I pulled myself upright. I dared not share that I worried about the unborn cowpuncher and instead put on proper cowgirl bravado. My doctor did not seem too concerned after he listened to the baby's heartbeat. "Just be careful," he cautioned and used to country folk, he said nothing about ending my riding activities. He was familiar with the ways of wives who had to pitch in with hard work on the farm.

Shane came into this world howling and kicking like a little broncobuster, or perhaps he was still protesting the rough ride he had for nine months. Shane first saw the light of day on a cool August morning, at the height of the dude season at Paradise Guest Ranch. He entered the world with the wind in the Rockies, under a cobalt blue sky above Pikes Peak. We had moved out of the fly invested feed lot to our dream home in the Rockies. The miracle dreamed about under the endless sky on the prairie had come true.

Wednesday night was a talent night when greenhorn guests and real cowboys and cowgirls sang, yodeled, acted out skids or made fools out of themselves. A mere week old, Shane became the youngest star of the show. I presented him on stage as the newest cowboy at Paradise Ranch. That night cheering guests and crew showered him with gifts that weren't exactly gifts of the magi, but did resemble gifts of the cowboy kind. There were gifts of hemp in the form of a hack rein. Gifts of fine cloth a la size 00 Levi-Strauss jeans. Gifts of subtle leather made into a pair of size 00 cowboy boots. Gifts of golden grains shaped into a straw cowboy hat and gifts of precious metals turned into a bit for a bridle. The gifts included intricate leathers in ornamental splendor, the chaps fitting a size zero-zero. Shane was all set to begin life the way it ought to be for a true cowpoke.

Opportunities to become a cowpoke for little crumb-cruncher Shane were numerous. Three days after his birth, mom couldn't stand to lounge around the house during the Sunday rodeo at the ranch. I packed up the little tyke in baby blankets and headed for the arena. The national anthem beckoned me to a dusty place where I had rounded up bulls, helped rodeo riders off their broncs and carried the American flag for the National Anthem. I placed the little tyke in the manger next to the arena as I watched the rodeo, feeling a bit left out because up until now I'd had always been in the limelight.

After the show, I was again in the limelight. Everyone wanted to have a peek at the pink—faced mini-cowboy. Perhaps the little tyke was in the limelight, not I, but I did not mind. Soon his new-baby preciousness would be fading and he might have to work to get attention instead of just lay there and do nothing. The little tyke cooperated like a trooper and seemed to enjoy his instant celebrity status. He peacefully slumbered in his new portable car seat. He never fussed and earned lots of remarks. "Gee, he's one quiet baby. What an angel."

Joe insisted that he already had the character of a cowboy.

He did however get so used to being fussed over that it didn't take him any time at all to figure out he was special. As he grew from a newborn tyke into a two-foot tall cowpoke, he continued to receive lots of attention. Seems adults adore little cowboys.

"Oh, ah," females twittered, "my, my, aren't you a handsome little man."

His size zero jeans had to be rolled up on the legs and the stiffness of the new denim caused him to appear bowlegged like some old grizzly cowpoke in the saddle for too long. Everyone fussed over him like a male Shirley Temple.

Shane learned to ride the ponies at the ranch as soon as he could walk and joined the children's counselors in the arena with the other guest kiddies. Unlike the guest children at the ranch, Shane got to ride mom and dad's horse now and then, a much higher distance from the ground than the guest children's ponies. He joined the young guests on picnics and rode the horse drawn coaches to the picnic area. In between the horsy fun, he swam in the Olympic pool and participated in games for the guest children supervised by ranch counselors. Summers at Paradise Ranch for Shane were like living in Disneyland. The difference between Shane and the guest kids was that Shane lived this Disneyland lifestyle all summer long while the guest children returned to their home in the city after a week.

After labor day, when the first leaves turned ochre, crimson and gold, the children's counselors, guests and most of the ranch crew packed their bags to return home or to another job someplace else. Fall spread its carpet of bright leaves over the hills and the ranch breathed a slower tempo. The ponies and most of the dude horses were turned out on mountain pastures. I hoisted Shane onto a real horse and watched him walk around and around the corral without help. He was not a bit worried about falling and just thought it was all great fun.

Off-season afforded more time to train horses. Shane's nanny departed for school and I, as the mother was now responsible for taking care of the little cowboy day and night. I invented ingenious ways to haul the little tyke along when working horses or traveling to a horse show or gymkhana. I brought a playpen to the rodeo arena, set it up, and placed the tyke in the pen with his favorite toys while riding my horse in the arena. The tyke appeared quite satisfied with his toys and all that fresh air. Shane didn't seem to mind that the fresh air was mixed with a bit of dust while the horse worked on racing barrels or learned how to stir up the dirt with sliding stops along the fence. I never contemplated that good ol' dirt and dust would hurt the little tyke as he had to get used to dust anyway if he was going to be a cowboy.

After Shane was born, the job at Paradise Guest Ranch boosted our confidence. We were someone besides drifters. We figured we were now respectable parents and carved out a permanent place in the community. With this new-found confidence, we reasoned, another little cowpoke might be the period to the question mark in our life. We would really be settled if the family grew to two kids. And perhaps I felt the crunch of time as I pushed thirty something, and perhaps this was my way of convincing myself that I belonged someplace on this earth and would have grandchildren in the wings when old age nipped at my heels.

Seeds of insecurity sprouted in the blissful soil of family once the first little cowpoke arrived. The question of 'what-about-the-rest-of-life' appeared as somber thoughts that had never entered my mind when we were not yet a family. The children were the anchors we needed to settle down and consider a life aside from drifting, new pastures and chasing adventure. Could we pull it off? I made myself believe in miracles.

Joe and I decided to take the plunge and give the little crumb-cruncher a brother or sister. At the same time, the cowboy tradition in Joe's family would be assured continuance. His grand daddy had been a cowboy, his daddy had been a cowboy, and this generation would continue the cowboy tradition into the next Millennium. I forgot to consider how the addition helped if father was unable to carry out the backbreaking work expected of a cowboy. Cowboy work is plagued by accidents, but I pushed that nagging apprehension out of my mind and thought that everyday would be a good day from now on.

"I'll be ridin' when I'm eighty." Joe joked. "By god, I probably have to."

With the second crumb-cruncher not yet seeing the light over the Colorado Rockies, I hoped the good days were not at the end of the fence line. The second pregnancy also remained a secret since I planned to ride without everyone advising me to stay home. I intended to continue riding and wrangling and managed to keep my secret throughout the summer. After all, I rode horses up to the day before Shane emerged. Surely, I thought, I could ride throughout the summer season with another little cowpoke tucked away behind a loose cotton shirt. No one appeared to suspect. I was lucky to gain very little weight and no one guessed as long as I wore loose shirts. Fine, I thought, I'll continue with riding lessons for the guests, leading rides into the rugged mountains below Pikes Peak and working as a pickup rider during our rodeos. My confidence in my horse and me had surpassed my caution and good sense.

Seventy-three was a good summer with only one disaster to cause concern. The whistle blew after eight seconds and Buck launched after the saddle bronc still bucking and trying to outrun both pickup horses. Buck's charge was abruptly halted by a fall to the ground, his front legs folding under his belly, his nose hitting the dirt and scooting up the arena sand. I instantly analyzed my dilemma. I was pregnant. My horse had hit the ground at a dead run, and what did I need to do keep the baby safe? Bail off? Stay on? Just then Buck regained some control and he righted himself. A leg at a time, he recovered into an upright position and continued charging after the bronc. All this happened within three or four second. We caught up with the bronc and no one was the wiser that I was a bit shook up.

In retrospect, my courage was most likely young ignorance, but I bravely and foolishly pushed the limits. My doctor informed me that it was fine for me to ride a horse, but I doubt he had that sort of riding in mind and certainly would never have condoned racing down a steep mountain, riding on precarious trails with cliffs and loose rocks, and chasing after broncs in rodeos. He probably would have locked me up and threw away the key, especially after hearing about the one particular escapade.

During the dude ranch season, Thursday evenings were reserved for the mountain outing. Guests learned to roll their bedrolls and rode to the top of the Rampard Range. After climbing on horseback to 10,000 feet with impressive vistas, the camp cook greeted guests and replenished their energy with sinfully thick steaks and heaps of potatoes fried on an open fire. Guests were treated with more than mouthwatering food. The spectacular view would stun even the spoiled traveler. Two thousand feet of vertical mountain plunged to the narrow valley Pikes Peak dominated the Southern sky. A few of us cowboys and girls who couldn't remain with the guests overnight after a gut filling cookout needed to ride back home before the night obliterated the narrow trails to the ranch. On one of those Thursdays, wrangler Tootie and Waddie Mitchell, two other wranglers and myself decided to race each other to the barns.

"I bet I can get there first." The challenge could not be ignored.

"Wanna' bet?" was the second challenge.

"Let's go!" sealed the challenge.

The racecourse was littered with obstacles of gullies, logs and rocks while plunging down the mountain at breakneck speed. Ping! Rocks catapulted under my horse's hoofs. Crunch! Twigs and pine needles were squashed as Buck bound over fallen tree trunks. The tyke inside somehow made it to the bottom with mom but he was probably unaware just how risky this ride had been to his well being. He also was not aware of the sweet taste of success as I skimmed the corner of the barn to end the race in a jolting stop to unsaddle my horse before the other racers arrived. Perhaps it was just as well that he could not see the sights or he might have howled with objections to such crazy stunts by his mother.

Travis entered this world in the depth of a Rocky Mountain winter with icicle appliqué along the roof of our home and below zero temperatures crystallizing the air. The ranch slept and there was plenty of time for a new baby.

Before the winter of his arrival, we contemplated a name. I wanted a special name.

"Different and meaningful," I pronounced. Casey, Joe, Drew, Andy? No, they weren't right.

During a chilly fall evening, Waddie Mitchell and his first wife Tootie discovered a name for the soon to be crumb-cruncher. Waddie is famous by now, a cowboy poet who brings laughter, tears and memories into many a cowpoke and greenhorn's life. Tootie followed her man to crazy places like a dude ranch and lived alongside of him with her own cowboy hat and spurs. Tootie suggested Travis and I knew it as the right name. Travis means he who comes to the cross-roads, a name that seemed befitting the newest cowpoke. He would someday have to choose which path to take. Follow the Hooper cowboy tradition or leave the range? We hoped his name would help him chose the right road.

He arrived on a blustery January morning, howling and kicking like the winds blustering off Pikes Peak. From the first breath of life, he objected to everything. A year passed and Travis was not accepting life without energetic howling. He seemed to respond to his parent's worries that Paradise Ranch was about to fall from grace. The ranch owners did not plan on another summer and soon filed for bankruptcy.

Our future again turned into a question mark. Dreams of security dissolved into worry and torment over how to make a living. We were asked to stay at the ranch to sell everything. We sold sixty draft horses and brass harness to match, two hundred head of riding horses with hundreds of saddles, two dozen horse drawn coaches, and the rodeo stock returned to Harry Vold Rodeo Company. We sat with stony faces as the gift shop's turquoise and silver jewelry sold. We bought silver and turquoise and Navajo rugs for a pittance, as an investment but more as a melancholy reminder of the great days of dude ranching. By spring, the barns, the lodge, and the rooms were stripped of summer charm. Chairs and sofas hovered beneath worn white sheets.

We were again without a home, a future and an income. Times were full of anxiety and the two little crumb-crunchers did not know what to make of their parent's worried brows.

Travis was to have none of the luxuries and the Disneyland existence his brother Shane experienced each summer. There were no more nannies, pony rides, trips in horse drawn coaches and frolicking in the Olympic size swimming pool. Hard times were once more knocking at the house and barn door. To us, hard time was not a stranger, but this time we had to think about a five year old and a one year old who needed a warm place, diapers and a world of security. Of course, the children were joined by the usual assortment of horses, dogs and cats that depended on us to keep warm and fed.

Joe worked in a mine until the right ranch job beckoned us to move. He found a position in Northern California on a cattle ranch that promised great visions toward management and fine housing and a place to raise a family. Searching for excitement was no more the primary driving force. A place to settle down to raise a family urged us into decisions we might not have made five years ago. "San Joaquin Valley might be a good place to raise 'em.," Joe said with conviction. "The school bus is supposed to come right to the ranch." I agreed, not convinced.

Visions of a fine new family home was promptly dispelled as we drove up to the ugly reality with a dilapidated house sweltering in hundred degree heat ebbing and flowing through the San Joaquin Valley day and night. Our vision and dream turned to dust billowing around the house with no lawns for the children, no cooling off at night, no social life, no neighboring children as companions for the two little cowpokes. The school bus to the ranch was a poor consolation. Travis was often so exhausted from the heat he fell asleep at the dinner table and Shane enrolled in Kindergarten but expressed his apprehension about riding down the dusty road to a strange school. He cried and said he wanted to leave.

It was past Halloween and signs of Christmas were appearing in the meager shop windows in Gustine. The children were not old enough to express their dissatisfaction in complete sentences, but they noted their parent's wrinkled brow, the hushed talks at night after a fourteen-hour day with meager pay. They sensed mom and dad's frustrations.

One evening I followed the little crumb-crunchers into their bedroom and discovered one entire wall scribbled and painted with crayons, but I saw no pictures of a child's imaginary art projects, only angry lines crossing the wall. I asked my oldest, whom I suspected of the deed, the usual question that parents ask.

"Why did you draw all over the wall?"

He answered in an unhappy squeaky voice. "I hate it here, mom". What was there to be angry about? We hugged instead with a shared sadness that barely soothes the soul.

"We hate it too." I assured him we would find someplace else. "We'll move soon. I promise. Your dad is going to find a good job on a real nice ranch." I hid my worry over how we were going to move anyplace. We were broke.

The real-soon happened shortly after the Shane's confession. Before Christmas, we moved to a happier place. Just as promised. The kids were excited and were not aware that we scraped together the last few dollars for another journey to a home we had never seen.

My vow to the kids that night of the wall scribble was not an idle promise. Happy Canyon ranch was paradise after the sharecropper's shack and the dusty yard that turned to mud with rains. At Happy Canyon, a lush yard with honeysuckle bushes and trees to climb appeared to be a fairyland for the two tykes. The little cowpokes were happy and content.

Shane liked his school and both kids remained in the same school district for the rest of their growing-up years. That is a feat for a cowboy who burns up the road to move to greener pastures sometimes faster than the grass can grow. For the next few years, there was happiness and bountiful hope for security. The security would not be shattered for years.

Again, rodeos, barbecues and friends occupied weekends. We could count on Halloween parties with costumes and Christmas with family and neighbors. Mom again started barrel racing and dad and mom were invited to ranches for roundups and branding. The little crumb-crunchers grew into capable young cowpokes riding the range. The horse trailer hauled horses to shows, rodeos and ranches. Every event turned into a family event.

After arrival at the horse show, I cleaned out the trailer, spread blankets on the floor, and deposited toys on the blanket while I barrel raced and visited. Travis never cried and turned into a trooper just like his brother when we hauled them to outings. The boys sat on lots of tall horses or their red cheeks were spotted peeking out of the door of the horse trailer while mom rode her horse or dad talked to other cowboys.

Soon Shane was in charge as caretaker and keeper of his younger brother. He took his job as seriously as cleaning the chicken house although he showed no more enthusiasm. A whining brother and pecking hens were similar. By the following spring, we advanced financially and bought a camper for the pickup that doubled as the portable babysitter whenever we were invited to a branding or round up, or just to stop at the local cowboy bar for a cool one after a long and dusty day. Life seemed on track for this cowboy family.

As the crumb-crunchers grew into their Levi jeans, they learned to hunt with their dad and roam the golden California hills. Travis was still a tad small, but he tagged along with his big brother. My faithful old Buck taught Shane and Travis how to work cattle but we thought it was time for the boys to ride their very own horse.

Fahra joined the family by accident. She was an unwanted pony and cost nothing but the transportation to the ranch.

"Don't look a gift horse in the mouth," I said, wondering why someone wanted to give away a beautiful pony. We figured we would find out soon enough why the owner wanted to find a home for the pony and reasoned she would not even make a dent in the hay supply and with her little squirt size, she'd be perfect for Shane and Travis. Fahra was a true pony, a real Shetland who reached just up to the belly of a normal horse. Her mane and tail dwarfed her tiny golden body and the voluminous amount of silver hair prompted the name Fahra Fawcett, a movie star in our time who stirred longings in every male with her generous blonde locks. Fahra was the kind of pony everyone wanted to take pictures of, but her beauty did not match her personality. As a typical ornery pony, she could outdo a mule in the department of pig-headedness. She kicked her hind heels up in protest to just about everything. If she agreed to leave the barn yard, her cooperation lasted only long enough until she arrived at her own personal perimeter where she suddenly changed from sluggishness to homebound agility, spinning one hundred and eighty degrees to run back to her corral. From time to time, I worked on a tune up. She objected to spurs and a bat, but finally Fahra gave in without a grandstand fuss. Her newly found obedience lasted a week after Shane rode her with apprehension, until she needed another tune up. Since I was small enough to ride her without dragging feet on the ground, the tune up tasks fell to me because Joe could just about stuff the pony in his hind pocket. Shane soon howled his disillusioned protest. "I don't wanna ride her," he whined, "I want a real horse."

Whenever I saddled the pony, Shane repeated his whining. "Do I have to? I don't wanna' ride her."

Like all cowboy parents, we figured Shane needed to get tough. A cowboy must learn to handle anything on four legs. "Go on, you'll be fine, just don't let her fool you."

Fahra knew the difference between a reluctant little boy and a mean adult cowgirl. Fahra bucked and ran backwards, sometimes dumping her reluctant rider. Eventually Shane was allowed to trade Fahra for big horses and someone charmed by her ravishing beauty adopted little Fahra.

Travis had been left in the dust when Shane learned to be a mini-cowboy. Travis, determined to be as adventurous as his big brother, refused to allow minor obstacles like fences to stop him from exploring. One early summer evening, Travis disappeared. He had been playing in the spacious yard surrounded by a six-foot mesh wire fence lined with honeysuckle and climbing rose bushes. As a mom with a sense of adventure the absence of one crumb cruncher did not seem worrisome. At first. There were lots of hiding places in the yard, but none revealed one little tyke. I checked outside the fence. Perhaps someone had left the gate open and Travis sneaked outside his confines? Perhaps his brother had taken him to the barn? I found no Travis in the ranch yard, the horse corrals, the barn, or the chicken house. Alone with no help to hunt the escapee, I widened the territory of my search. Panic gripped my throat. I switched into high gear and alert mode. The little whippersnapper was after all only three years old. I checked all the places once more, hoping I overlooked a hiding place, thinking up a reasonable explanation why I could not find Travis and remembering the time he turned up missing from our house in Colorado where I finally discovered him at the horse corral. The nine months old twerp had scooted three hundred yards up a bumpy slope and sat by the fence, without a tear, a bit perplexed by his mountain expedition. This time Travis was more mobile with two extra years under his mini cowboy belt. Where could his mobility take him? What dangers could he encounter? The creek? A hungry mountain lion or bobcat? Ruminating about dangers, I spotted a lone bull way out in a yellowing field past the house, a huge hunk of black Angus, engulfed in a cloud of dust rising from his pawing hoofs. In front of the bull sat little Travis. The danger had not been mountain lions or bobcats, the danger was a ton of black flesh pawing the ground, head shaking with snot flying from his nostrils. For one moment, and only a moment, I froze before I raced through the field to rescue my youngest. I snatched him off the ground, eyeing the bull still pawing and throwing snot, but he seemed to have no interest in the frantic mother and the little bundle she snatched off the ground.

A closer inspection of the yard revealed a handy hole dug under the fence, most likely scratched and scraped by one of the dogs. Travis had wasted no time taking advantage of the escape route to explore the rest of the world. His tear stained face caked with dust and his choked sobs revealed that he seemed more than ready to return to his fenced world.

There were other incidents. Falls from horses, cuts and bruises, poison ivy, pecked hands from angry chickens, and ticks. Ranch life was the teacher to prepare our little cowboys for the future.

On the ranch, there were no drugs, no gangs, cars to dodge on busy streets or time on a child's hands to stir up trouble. Ranch life meant learning how to work hard, with chores for everyone. The boys learned to take responsibility for the animals when they were just tiny tykes. Shane had grown barely past his daddy's knees when he rode along to feed cattle. After he grew tall enough to reach his daddy's belt, he drove the pickup while dad threw out hay for the cows. He had to kneel on the seat, but in low gear and the accelerator jammed by a stick of wood, Shane proudly steered the pickup through fields and over hills.

Travis and Shane were well indoctrinated to chores and beasts that didn't give a peck about behaving. Cleaning the chicken house was the boy's least favorite chore. Collecting the eggs ranked second. The cranky old hens maliciously pecked at little hands when they reached into the nests.

"Do I have to?" They whined when reminded to clean the chicken house on Saturday.

The answer remained the same. "Just go do it. You'll be all right." The money earned for cleaning the chicken house was their consolation.

As time passed, the little cowpokes grew up into young men who loved their ranch life and their old cowpoke dad, but they also learned being a cowboy is a tough life on this earth. They wanted more than worrying about bills, dusty days filled with cold or heat or mud, and the insecurity of a drifter's life. The boy's who grew up as little cowpokes turned away from the cowboy legacy that their dad had carried on from his father, his grandfather, and great grandfather. As the modern world showed less use for the cowpoke and his way of life, the time had come to choose a road away from the traditional cowboy life. Perhaps Waylon Jennings' message has a measure of truth:

"Cowboy's ain't easy to love.

They'd rather give you a song than diamonds and gold

Mammas don't let your babies grow up to be cowboys

Don't let 'em pick guitars and ride them old trucks

Let 'em be doctors and lawyers and such."

Shane and Travis might not ride them old trucks and spent their workdays on horses, but the boys carried on the most precious of gifts from the cowboy way of life. Integrity, a love for animals, and toughing out the problems in life.

6

The Halcyon Days

The Halcyon days were the prosperous years, the fat years wedged between a cowboy's lean times. Those were the years that triumphed over worries, poverty knocking at the door, and unrealized dreams of greener pastures.

Paradise Guest Ranch was our lush pasture. Unlike many other jobs on ranches, the pasture remained green and did not wither or dry up with weeds and locoweed. The Paradise pasture sprouted not just green grass, but laughter, adventure, security, glamour and excitement. Years at Paradise Ranch were like a string of pearls with each pearl a bright tale of bliss and thrills that I would not trade for a dozen trips around the world.

Luxury was part of the ranch life at Paradise, the exclusive bright star on the dude ranch horizon. Living and working at the ranch resembled suspiciously close to living in a fairytale world.

Where else could a horse-crazy girl and her cowpoke husband find four hundred head of horses, many of them topnotch mounts from a dozen breeds? And where else could you hitch up several eight-up teams and choose matched teams from among sixty Percheron, Shire and Belgian draft horses? Fairytales of course have coaches. Cinderella might have been jealous of the line up of twenty-five restored wagons. Brewster stagecoaches from New York, a surrey with the fringe on top, a streetcar enclosed with etched glass, Conestoga wagons and Budweiser style beer wagons, buckboards, coaches and phaetons. In fairytale land there are a few Hollywood dreams come true. Chariots from the first Ben Hur movie with freshly gilded wheels waited for wild-eyed teams hitched four abreast. They kicked up the dust in the rodeo arena for the weekly rodeo. For the rodeo cowboy as well as wide eyed Eastern greenhorns, first rate Harry Vold rodeo stock promised chills, spills and thrills every Sunday for the summer season. The guest's kiddies were not forgotten. They too lived in fairytale land for a week with their own ponies, their own coaches and drivers.

The Old Man

Paradise Guest Ranch hired two hundred summer hands to care for the welfare and whims of two hundred pampered guests. Twenty-five wranglers worked seven days a week during the summer with hundreds of horses and guests.

Jobless and drifting to Colorado from the Canadian Northwest, Joe found his first dude ranch job at Paradise Ranch when he still dreamed that a cowboy could make a living with a saddle, his rodeo bag and a satchel of clothes. The next time he returned he brought a wife. Many a cowboy had been enticed back to this western fantasy world much like a cowboy might be drawn to the sweetness of a fresh can of Skoal. When Paradise ranch offered Joe the foreman position after our miserable flyspecked existence at the feedlot, Joe promised his young wife that this would become our haven and the green pasture he dreamt about. Paradise Ranch did become our paradise for nine years. Never mind that the nine years were split into three years with a hitch in California before coming back for another six years. Nine years any which way you look at it, is a long time for an itchy cowboy who can't get it out of his blood that more thrills and better cowboyin' is just over the hill.

Cowboys and a few adventurous cowgirls brought their saddles and a bag full of clothes to hire on as wranglers. They traveled from the Far West, the North and the South for a summer of fun and riding. They were unaware that the man who owned Paradise Ranch fancied himself as God and dictated purity and obedience to his summer crew. Frank Snell was an ornery old cuss in his eighties, and not about to bow to anyone. He was the supreme ruler maker, and the enforcer with the iron grip. Snell hammered the rules on a stone much like the Ten Commandments, and expected Joe to carry them out. Old man Snell of course got older, and with each birthday, he got meaner. The meaner and more unreasonable he got, the more paranoid he became. He collected a few dozen enemies along the way.

In 1965, old man Snell could get away with his shenanigans. He apparently had never heard of anti slave laws. In the sixties, ranchers figured that as long as they paid a man his wages, they upheld the law and could tell a man how to pull on his Levis. Old man Snell figured as long as he signed the paycheck, he owned that person twenty-four hours a day and could dictate his waking and sleeping hours. He also figured that he needed to be a single-handed savior of sinful behaviors, suspecting that every one of his two hundred employees was capable of imaginable and unimaginable sin. Since all employees lived under Frank Snell's bunkhouse roofs, the man was capable of enforcing his fire and brimstone rules and rid his patch of earth from sin. Snell's office sat high up in the main lodge overlooking the barns, the men's bunkhouses, and the rodeo arena. Thankfully, he could not scrutinize the girl's bunkhouse because it hid in the woods behind the lodge, but he figured that females were not as tempted as males to commit sin. Cowboys in particular were most likely to engage in amoral behavior. From his throne, he ruled with an ironclad hand, and whenever Frank Snell called Joe or me to the office, we knew he suspected somebody had broken Snell's law. Old man Snell also patrolled the ranch in his ostentatious Cadillac Eldorado to check out places he could not examine from his throne. Frank, of course, could never be called Frank. His name remained Mr. Snell to everyone. Nobody messed with Mr. Snell. If we objected to enforcing his rules, we would have been shown the front gate without further ado.

Every male and female, whether they were a server, a kitchen helper, a maid, a barn boy, wrangler or blacksmith were to be in bed by ten at night. Fraternization between male and female employees was forbidden, so was fraternization with the opposite sex guests, which made for a summer of absolute temptation as scores of female guests traveled West to meet the cowboy of their dreams. Some arrived dreaming of a romance, some settled for a one or two-night stand and others wandered West with marriage in mind. One-night stands were readily available if the female dude was willing to consummate her dreams in a bedroll. Female employees were another source of temptation to the cowboys. The women employees, a good quarter of the crew, were forbidden to wander to the men's accommodations. The old man knew his business when he built the female bunkhouse on one side of the highway, and the men's bunkhouse on the other. A highway separated the barn and bunkhouse from the lodge, guest accommodations and female quarters. The women were not allowed on the barn side and were just as much under Snell's law. On the other hand, female guests could not be subject to such scrutiny.

Serious fraternizing had to be accomplished after lights-out and after random bed checks. If God detected any romantic, outright sexual or non-sexual fraternization, Joe or I were required to immediately fire the sinners. If God suspected sexual activity, the wrath of the entire Victorian morals cast their spell upon the guilty souls. Frank Snell never hinted of clues as to his abhorrence for intimate fraternization. We could only make up with wild guesses. Conversations with close friends attempted to solve the mystery.

"I think the old lady played around on him." Buddy guessed. "Maybe she played around a might too much. Just look at her pictures. She was kind a' pretty."

Tom agreed. "I bet she had an affair with a cowboy at the ranch, now ol' Frank's gettin' back at everybody."

Reggie had a different idea. "I think he's the one who had affairs. Those guys always preach what they sinned about."

Perhaps Snell knew first hand about the sins of youth from his own juvenile days, although we had a difficult time imagining the old man as a young romantic rascal with hot pants.

"Hell no," Tom thought of a different reason, "he's jealous 'cause he can't do it anymore."

The rumors started afresh every summer. We did not dare ask the old man and could only speculate. Perhaps in Snell's senior years, ruling two hundred souls were his only way of getting a high out of life.

Both Joe and I craved the opulence, the security and the thrills of the job after the fly-specked feed lot in Eastern Colorado and figured we could put up with the old man's whims.

The first summer that Joe hired on as foreman, Joe and I were required to fire sixty employees in three months. Toward the end of the season, the pickings were slim. Finding someone who would not only work their rear end off but also hold to virginal values was no small task. We tried to turn a blind eye to most shenanigans that remained well covered in the dark and behind Snell's back, especially with a few experienced wranglers, coach drivers and blacksmiths, who were difficult to replace. The average wrangler and barn-boy passed through the gates one week and passed through those same gates walking the opposite way the next week.

In response to the Victorian expectations, sex and youth, particularly if combined, wranglers had no limit as to inventing creative ways to meet for clandestine twosomes, a few drinks or worse yet, dancing in a local establishment, considered brothels by the old man. Snell even created patrols to these local brothels to inspect them for any attempts by cowboys to infiltrate them secretly on a Saturday night.

Joe busied himself elsewhere when he knew someone's pants got a little hot for a fine looking Eastern dude. He also knew where the wires in the fence were most stretched because of the traffic sneaking out at the back of the ranch. He ignored the obvious. When the wanton behavior became too obvious and the back fence got stretched too far, Joe dropped a hint that he knew something was up and the cowboys slowed down their clandestine activities for a few days or found a new place in the fence. Since Woodland Park was a mere mile from the Ranch, the temptations of bars, drinks and dancing were too enticing to ignore. Occasionally, a snitch among the wranglers who hoped to dethrone Joe or his assistant or some other favored cowboy, would let slip to old man Snell that he spotted so and so at a place of sin in town or not in bed by ten at night. Joe would then be questioned why he did not know about this incident, and ordered him to fire the perpetrator immediately. Joe fired the poor cowboy, knowing that if he objected, the perpetrator would be fired anyway and most likely, both of us would lose our job and our home in the process.

The cowboys, most in a stage of perpetual ecstasy, ogled the eastern girls arriving each week. A new batch of young female dudes arriving was nearly as exciting as a new batch of horses arriving. Since dudes rarely remained more than one week, the cowboys needed to work fast. That left precious few nights or days time to start a relationship. The cowboys were innovative, and hurried the romance as quickly as possible. They fluffed and padded their beds for the bed check, they reported an inordinate number of car problems when driving to town in the early evening, and bribed their way out of rules.

I also dutifully performed my assignment as the warden with the female employees. My job was to keep the girls on the north side of the ranch, away from the bunkhouses on the south side of the ranch, but a few exceptions existed. Female employees were allowed to walk to the South side to clean men's lodging and the bunkhouses for those men who were willing to pay a small fee, but the cowboy's bunkhouse in the large hip roofed barn had been designated as an off-limit establishment. Why Snell thought the girls could earn a few dollars cleaning a dishwasher and waiter's quarters but not the cowboy quarters had never been discussed. Speculations were rampant. On rodeo day, the south side opened to the public and became an open Mecca for female employees.

As a married woman and a wrangler, I was allowed the run of the ranch. Married to the foreman and being a female wrangler brought status the other girls did not enjoy.

The last five years at Paradise Ranch, after God's retirement, the dude ranch existed despite relaxed rules and despite the lack of a morality patrol. Old man Snell retired with his wife to Florida and disappeared from his Wild West kingdom. Texas oil people bought and liberated the ranch. Wranglers were now allowed in the bar and were even expected to socialize with the guests. Bed checks were non-existent, and the new owners ignored quickie romances with pretty eastern dudes who made eyes at a cowboy. Old man Snell probably would have had a heart attack had he known his Paradise turned into a sinful Garden of Eden.

The Cowboys

The characters hired as wranglers, wagon drivers, blacksmiths and barn boys were a unique breed and added soul and spirit to each summer. They ranged from lusty young men to grizzly old codgers to experienced horsemen and wannabe cowboys.

Reginald had been hired as wrangler a month before we arrived at the ranch from the fly specked feed lot. Reginald was a summer cowboy, the kind who drifts to two or three jobs a year, not particularly ambitious, but adored by the guests because of his charm. He wormed his way into the heart of female dudes with a toothy smile under his dusty hat brim. He was a lanky and bony specimen, his long legs bowed and skinny as the hind legs of a spider. We never did remember his last name. He agonized over the blemishes on his face. He picked and scratched and bought salves and lotions, but could not get rid of his dreaded zits. Reginald earned the nickname of Reginald von Zitt. Good natured, he ignored his nickname, and hoped that a few zits were not going to cost him the longed for romances with starry-eyed female guests from Chicago or New York. The zits apparently did not interfere with a sufficient number of romances. With the male-female ratio in favor of the cowboys even if they presented a picture of fewer charms once they removed their hats or Levis, Reginald landed his share of romantic encounters. The starry eyed Easterners did not notice that his rangy frame slouched on his horse that always seemed too short for him. Despite the lack of Hollywood cowboy semblance, Reginald zeroed in on a fresh girl each week. He didn't say much when his fellow cowboys teased him, but bragged just enough to let them know he could score just as well as anyone. "She's a looker. Mighty fine. Mighty fine." Reginald grinned and left the rest to the imagination.

Stoney Martin was another rangy character but he did not have to worry about zits and looked just a bit handsomer than Reginald. Compared to Reginald's swarthy dark complexion, Stoney impressed the Ladies with his golden locks and baby blue eyes. He did compete with Reginald as the skinniest cowboy on the ranch. Stoney also belonged to the world of drifters. Stoney's calm, cool cowboy charm and his lean weathered face framed by his beat up silver-belly cowboy hat pulled way down over his brows was a magnet for female guests. His crooked smile with a few missing teeth were no deterrent when his baby blues settled on a girl. His limbs were like willow branches, and his bowed legs betrayed a number of years in the saddle. With his dry wit and toothy humor, Stoney was never shy of girl friends or for that matter, friends. He found nothing aversive, no one an enemy and everything in life could be turned into a comedy. He bantered and teased his way through the day. He loved all women but searched for someone to share his life. Stoney collected wives when others collected girlfriends. Stoney returned to the ranch for several summers and one summer he managed to marry twice. "She's a foxy lady," he grinned, "we're gonna settle down this fall." The settling down never materialized.

During Stoney's first summer at the ranch, he planned the marriage as an extra special event. He did not object for a moment when a starry eyed Chicago lady chose him to be her man and dreamed of being a cowboy's wife. The wedding took place during a Sunday rodeo. Stoney and his bride wanted to marry cowboy style. The bride, groom, witnesses, and preacher gathered in the arena with an especially mild mannered mount for the preacher. The event happened during the last of the dude ranch years after old man Snell sold his Paradise and retired to Florida. The spectators loved the extravaganza and the notion of romance in the rodeo arena. The fairytale beginning in the rodeo arena faded as quickly as it had blossomed. A month later, Stoney's bride experienced the pinches of being a cowboy's wife and decided her dream cowboy was not Prince Charming after all. She packed her bags and hurried back to Chicago. Stoney grinned through his couple of missing teeth. "She just got homesick, ah well."

Stoney did not mourn his lost bride for long and wrangled himself another honey. This time the bride insisted on a church wedding in the nearby city of Colorado Springs complete with parents and a wedding shower. Stoney thought that was a lot of hullabaloo, but he humored his bride with the same crooked smile he used for all of life's little problems. The time was fall, the ranch had closed its doors for the season and the last of the cowboys gathered their saddles to move on. Stoney wrangled himself a winter job at the ranch to cut wood and repair saddles, wagons, and fences to support his new bride. This marriage lasted a few months until his bride felt just as disillusioned as Betty and she too packed her bags and hurried back to Chicago. Stoney was again a free spirit.

'That's just the way it goes," he said. After Stoney left Paradise Ranch, he married a lady smitten with the cowboy way of life. She stayed around longer than the others, putting up with liquor, carousing and moving to a ranch without electricity. She reaped his compliments for her steadfastness. "I found me one fine woman."

Long after Paradise Ranch closed its doors for the last time, we received a telephone call from Stoney's latest bride. She cried when she related the bad news that Stoney drowned in a flooded river after his pickup had been swept away by strong currents. His favorite dog was with him. Stoney had represented one of those cowboy characters especially created by God to make the West a special place.

The old Ogallala Sioux traveled all the way from the Dakotas, hoping for a job to support himself through the summer. He appeared on a cool and blustery spring day, his face weather stained and carved by time, and no one knew his age. His leathery face bespoke of silent pride and wisdom. Sometimes he emanated sadness and his eyes were far off in the distance. He never complained, never criticized, he just wanted a job and said to call him Crazy Horse. We figured his real name was something else, but what did it matter? The name added mystique to dude ranch life, and fascinated Easter greenhorns. Joe called him 'Chief' out of respect and deference to his age, his status and experience, and hired him as a wagon driver. Crazy Horse enjoyed the 'Chief' part and we guessed that he hadn't been important for a long time. The Chief said he could drive anything with four legs hitched to a set of wheels; and sure enough, Crazy Horse knew how to hitch a team, talk to them through the lines, and was one of those rare men who knew how to manage eight-ups.

The Chief also knew how to play the eastern greenhorn game. He wore Indian-style white man clothing, just like in the many pictures of Buffalo Bill's Wild West show: A vest, a flat brimmed hat, his long silver hair in braids. He spoke in short sentences, a la Hollywood style, with a knowing twinkle that never left his eyes. "How. Good day for wagon ride." Or he announced: "No good day for wagon ride." He kept his thoughts to himself.

Crazy Horse diligently collected horsehair, and stole some from the tails of horses that had particularly long tails. Instead of chasing after women, liquor and parties, Crazy Horse spent his free time braiding the hair into hatbands, belts and bolo ties. His gift to me was a black and white hatband and he said he figured it would be just right for my silver belly Tom Mix hat. "This go real good with your hat, young lady."

I figured that he figured right.

The summer Crazy Horse hired on as wagon master, it rained and rained, often for days on end. The heavens above Pikes Peak growled and thundered and refused to shut their floodgates. The rain dampened the enthusiasm of the guests and minor complaints turned into major grumbling. Not only dudes complained, but also the wranglers. They rode on wet saddles and boots that never dried before the next day's use. If you did not own a second pair of boots to interchange with the wet ones, life turned a bit moldy and uncomfortable. The Cowhand, the local western store, however, profited handsomely by selling slickers and plastic hat covers. The Chief's major mission that summer was to end the relentless rain. Crazy Horse promised he could do something about the wet plague and invoke the gods to shut off the faucet.

"Ai,ai,ai…ai,   ai-ai-ai,   how,how,how,how,…how-how…"   Crazy Horse chanted before the wranglers woke to another gray morning. Long before most normal humans were out of bed, Crazy Horse danced and chanted his 'no rain-um dance' as the first light of morning bathed the barnyard. Most of the time, the gods must have forgotten Crazy Horse and ignored him. Instead, the old Sioux chants and his time-honored dance brought the cowboys out of bed before the alarm clock rang. The Chief created a magic that spellbound even the most cynical cowboy and invoked thoughts of those long lost days when the West was wild and real instead of make belief. We wondered if the Chief also longed for those bygone days.

After the summer, Crazy Horse disappeared. We never did know his real name. We never knew where he traveled to but all of us wished he would some-day be happy even if it had to be in his happy hunting grounds.

Waddie Mitchell became a legendary cowboy poet many years after his dude ranch summer, but Waddie had to pay his dues before he could recite his poems to the world. Joe hired Waddie one early spring with patches of snow still loiter-ing in the shade, just as the horses were brought back to the ranch and needed their tune up before the dudes descended on Paradise Guest Ranch. Waddie could do just about anything. Drive a wagon, shoe a horse, and cuss with the best. He belonged to the species of genuine Nevada cowpoke. He portrayed the image down to the Skoal can in his rear pocket. He looked like the sort of cow-boy who should grace the pages of a coffee-table book about cowboys and he cer-tainly fit right into the Wild West image at Paradise Ranch. Waddie wore a big 'Hoss type' cowboy hat, he wouldn't be without his silk scarf around his neck, and his boots with high under-slung heels covered his jeans up to the knees. Even for a young man, Waddie had already acquired the correct bow to his legs, but he was also young enough the sun had not yet etched his baby soft face. More than one female eastern dude found her heart skipping several beats, but Waddie avoided chasing pretty city gals. With a wife like Tootie, the city gals lost out. Tootie was the female carbon copy of her husband. Broad ten gallon hat, the scarf neatly tied around her neck, and a hint of bowlegged jeans stuffed into high topped fancy cowboy boots with those same high under-slung heels. Waddie and Tootie were always exceptionally clean. They managed to smell clean even around horses, so clean they looked like they just got dressed for a photo shoot. Even when Waddie shod horses, he managed to wear an immaculately pressed cotton shirt, topped off by a silk scarf. Tootie also managed to appear crispy clean and neater than the rest of the crew, with the freshly scrubbed look of a cowgirl planning a day in town with her honey.

Waddie came straight from the Nevada desert where cowboys don't see a lot of people and deal with cows and steers, the weather and a few coyotes. He was a greenhorn about dude ranch life, and while his wife Tootie had to deal with people as a wrangler, Waddie often hid away from dudes and thought it just swell that he could hang out behind the barn at the blacksmith shop. Dudes were not allowed behind the huge hip-roofed barn and Waddie could cuss up a storm when he needed to relieve his true feelings toward a horse that refused to cooperate. "You blasted s…o…b! Sonofabitch! Sh…! Damned, get OFF of me! You rotten sh…! Some days, one could hear plenty of interesting words. If Tootie wanted to use the same words some days with plain dumb or demanding guests from the city, she had to hold her tongue and smile. The draft horses that leaned or sat on Waddie while he held up a foot, or the cantankerous riding mount that attempted to kick Waddie to the next barn weren't bothered by his cuss words.

Waddie helped wrangle dudes only when absolutely necessary. Dudes were not Waddie's forte. He preferred running bovine critters on a million-acre Nevada spread. Dudes talked back, they couldn't be roped when they complained. Waddie put on his tolerant face and helped guide the dudes on their mountain rides. I doubt we can repeat what he thought.

Despite Eastern dudes who talk back instead of moo, mean horses that tried to kill Waddie when he shod them, a meager salary, the cowpoke and his cowgirl wife survived the summer.

While Waddie was a dyed in the wool cowpoke, another person hankered to become one. During the mayhem weeks of spring, Joe tried to discourage and get rid of a pesky red headed character that said his name was Tom Collins, but Tom stuck around like honey on flypaper. We thought a skinny and freckled kid like Tom would soon give up when the chips were down, but Tom surprised everyone. He was a wannabe cowboy, wet behind both ears and had never ridden much of anything except a few backyard horses. He showed up early one spring and applied for a job as wrangler. Joe had no intention to hire a little whippersnapper with no cowboy experience. "I'm looking for experienced cowboys," Joe flat out told him "I just don't have time to break somebody in." That deterred Tom about as much as a yellow jacket honing in on a piece of meat after the citronella candle is extinguished.

Tom wanted to be a cowboy in the worst way and he thought that he could be one by just wanting it bad enough. At least he had been honest and said he had no experience with horses or livestock and didn't have a clue how to be a wrangler but in the same breath added that he could learn to be a cowboy in a few days. Joe lectured to him. "I expect the wranglers to know how to ride anything with four legs. You gotta know how to gentle a crazy killer horse. Gotta know how to rope anything that's got ears or horns. Gotta know how to work with rodeo stock that wants to stomp ya into the dust. Gotta know how to doctor a sick horse or Brahman bull and not let 'em eat you." Then Joe added, "A wrangler's got to be real nice to guests and bring each and every one of them home in one piece even if they're loco as hell or ride lopsided on a horse that walks crooked on a six inch trail next to a hundred foot cliff." The job description did not budge Tom from his mission.

He said "No problem, I'm gonna be the best cowboy alive. And by the way," he added, "I also want to be a bronc rider." Tom's dreams were mighty, but Joe still had no intention to hire a snot-nosed kid with dreams as his experience.

Joe turned Tom away for the twentieth time without discouraging the kid with the red freckles. A week later he checked in again. Like a fly he buzzed back again a week later. As the ranch pace increased during late spring, Tom Collins's red mop of hair appeared more often. The horses had been rounded up from their mountain winter pastures. Fresh batches of dude horses had been purchased at auctions by the semi loads. April and May was the month when horses were shod, vaccinated, roped, hobbled, saddled, the buck rode clear out of their hides, their training tuned up, the worst of the worst culled to ship back to auctions, and the rodeo stock collected for the summer. New wranglers were traditionally assigned the worst horses with the most buck and the nastiest habits. By May, most of the wranglers had been hired and the ranch kitchens fired up to feed the early crew. Anticipation warmed the chill in the air whipping off Pikes Peak, cussing colored the breaking in period of the horses; and just as often, after a long winter of roaming the prairie and mountain pastures, horses tried to break in the wranglers instead of wranglers trying to break the horses.

Tom increased his pesky appearances, and didn't just come by once a week but loitered around the barns daily and generally made a pest of himself. Joe finally took pity on the kid who wanted so badly to become a cowboy and hired him under certain conditions. "Hell, ok, I'll hire you but you gotta show you can ride."

Tom, exuding confidence, moved his bedroll and brand new cowboy duds into the bunkhouse. The next morning, horses were assigned to the wranglers to ride until they were considered gentle and safe dude horses. The drill was the same every morning. Before breakfast, a hundred or 200 head of horses were run into the rodeo arena, and the chosen ones chased into the round corral. From the round corral, they were led to their open ended stalls. Grain boxes in each stall were already filled and the aroma of hay permeated the stalls. At first, there was mayhem. Horses milled about, bit and kicked each other and sometimes a wrangler, clouds of dust billowed into the cold sky, and whinnies pierced the cold morning when best friends were separated. Within days, the horses learned to walk to their own stalls without human escort as they were released from the round corral. Within two weeks most horses identified their own stalls and were happy to oblige. If one of the horses entered the wrong stall, they were kicked out immediately by the rightful owner. Once the horses were tied, curried, saddled and munching their breakfast, the wranglers were served their respective breakfast at the employee dining room. A hardy breakfast of pancakes, eggs, bacon, slabs of ham and home fries were well deserved after saddling over a hundred horses and harnessing two dozen draft horses.

Tom's first morning was his test. Joe assigned him a small white horse that looked like a mangy overgrown pony and instructed Tom about his assignment. "All right, you warm the horse up before you come to breakfast. Ride 'em till he ain't bucking anymore."

Tom complied with greenhorn enthusiasm. He did not notice the currycomb and the burr that somehow founds its way securely attached to the cinch. Tom led his horse off to the rodeo arena while the rest of the cowboys headed for the dining room to fortify their stamina with hot chow.

Tom never did show up for breakfast. After breakfast the cowboys walked back to the barns and noted that Tom was still astride that little white horse, and the little white horse still tried to buck now and then, although the attempts were half hearted by now. Tom figured correctly that he had better stay on top of the horse until the horse turned into a gentle child's pony. When he finally did get off the horse, Tom found the bur under the blanket and the currycomb attached to the cinch. Tom said nothing. He passed his initiation.

One particular busy week, Tom earned a most undesired fame, primarily among guests although the cowboys delighted in repeating the story to anyone who would listen for the rest of the summer. Guest rides at Paradise Ranch were often fifty to over a hundred dudes on each ride and needed attendance by wranglers in front, one in back and along the flank to shepherd the dudes along mountain trails. That memorable week a number of employees and guests contracted Montezuma's revenge.

The problem was soon solved, and the faulty dishwasher repaired and food served again on meticulously rinsed dishes. Before the rinse cycle had been repaired, a certain kind of institutional soap scum remained on the plates, cups, glasses and silverware. Although the problem lasted only one day, the scum resulted in phenomenal reactions. Many guests elected to remain close to the facilities. There were the hardy guests, particularly the young ones who were a bit tougher when it comes to intestinal revolt. Those hardy guests showed up at the barn to sign up for rides, and by chance or good luck, many of them happened to be pretty girls from the East.

Some of the wranglers were also hardy but a few were severely afflicted. Afflicted or not, the wranglers had little choice but to ride and hope for the best. Once the ride left the barnyard, there were no facilities. Tom had contracted the terrible revenge, and figured that he was much too macho to succumb to it. "No respecting cowboy messes his pants when he's on a horse," Tom bragged. However, Montezuma must have forgotten to exempt cowboys. The urge struck Tom about half way through the ride. Tom figured even if there were no facilities, there were plenty of bushes and trees to shelter the necessary operation and one could disappear unnoticed for a few moments. Tom dropped to the back of the ride, excusing himself from the pretty girls whom he tried to impress. By now, he had to get the job done pronto and rode his horse behind a large dogwood bush. That day Tom happened to be riding the little white horse, the same one who bucked for an hour on his initiation day. Although he had been cursed with riding the little white horse more days then he would have chosen, Tom felt he had been successful with his training attempts. He expected the little white horse to behave himself as he cleverly hid behind the cluster of dogwoods. He dropped his pants before it was too late, and crouched down. The little white horse hated being left behind, or perhaps he had been spooked by Tom's hasty departure to the bush or perhaps the little pony hadn't been trained as well as Tom believed. In any case, the little white horse jumped out from behind the bush and did his best to bolt back to the other horses before Tom could pull up his pants. Tom kept a good grip on the reins since letting go of the horse would have meant he'd walk all the way back to the barn. No cowboy wants to ever experience such an embarrassment. Tom stubbornly dug in his heels, at the same time, desperate to finish the necessary job and not be yanked out from behind the dogwood bush. The little horse had Tom by a decided disadvantage, dragging Tom out from his cover with every dude of course aware of the commotion, checking out the situation. A few choice words "#*^#>*" completed the disaster.

Tom tried his best to remain anonymous for the rest of the week and desperately attempted to hide whenever the pretty girls on that fateful ride appeared at the barn. The little white horse had moved to number one on Tom's blacklist.

That fall, we sold the little white horse at an auction. He continued his unpredictable behavior, buck whenever he pleased at the worst times and spooked routinely. He was just a notch too stubborn and ornery for a dude horse. Tom relished getting rid of him so he the foremen could not make him ride the crazy little horse the next summer. At the horse auction, Joe decided that Tom would probably get mad at the little horse if he rode him into the auction ring, and blow the chances of bringing a fair price. The boys elected me to ride the little critter since buyers in the audience would surely believe he was a nice little horse if a girl rode him. He did not bring much of a profit, but the sale to some other sucker pleased Tom immensely.

The Wild, Wild, Wild West

By the mid-twentieth century, most of the real Wild West ended up pressed between the pages of books. Shoot-outs at the OK corral or on a dusty main street belonged to history. Rodeos were tamed into highly structured entertainment managed by college educated contractors. The one hundred-dollar horse had become obsolete, replaced by the thousand-dollar mount with a pedigree from here to there. All inclusive packages for city slickers at dude ranches included tamed down rides, and the West was presented to dudes in a watered down, domesticated version.

Not so at Paradise Ranch. At Paradise you could still experience the occasional runaway or wagon wreck, a wild version of rodeo, a fugitive hiding from the law and working as a cowpoke, and even shoot outs. Wranglers were characters who ranged from 'wannabe's, to genuine cowpoke characters with few possessions but a saddle and a pickup. Some cowboys were fresh off vast cattle outfits with cow camps. Buffalo McCormick spent his life drifting between dude ranches and cattle outfits. When Buffalo tired of cows he switched to dudes for a summer. At summer's end, Buffalo was ready to hit the range and deal with bovine problems instead of dude problems. Other hired hands at the barn were rodeo riders, still others trained horses and a select few were experienced teamsters. A few assorted barn boys, wranglers and swampers, teamster's helpers and manure shovelers were of dubious character. True to the old Wild West, nobody asked questions. As long as the hired hand kept his nose clean, worked without complaining from dawn to dusk, treated guests with civility, ride any creature with a tough hide and four legs and followed old man Snell's rules, a man's history was inconsequential.

If the previous qualifications were not met, the man soon packed his bags. The fired employee had to gather his belongings within the hour, turn in his bedding and towels before Joe drove him to the bus station if he didn't have his own transportation. The rule was to get the fired person off the ranch pronto to avoid revenge. Cowboys resented being firing when their only sin had been drinking at a local bar or sneaking into the ranch after bedtime. Some didn't take kindly to being fired for good reasons. The dubious characters were rushed off the ranch before they could properly close their suitcase.

This is where the story of the shoot out begins. One of the barn boys hired during mid summer appeared to be a shifty character, but barn boys were in short supply by the time the time summer reached its apex. As was customary, the shifty character hired on with no questions asked. Hiring procedures consisted of describing his job. Joe clearly described the duties.

"Ok, you're gonna clean all the stalls and the yard after the rides leave. When they get back in the afternoon, you clean again. Got that? I got one man driving the wagon and you throw the manure in. If you learn how to drive a horse, you can trade off with the driver."

The new man agreed to accept the job as a poop shoveler, although saddling and feeding horses would bring relief to endless shoveling after several hundred horses left their mark. The new man started his job then and there. Sometimes less than an hour would pass from the time a man walked through the front ranch gate to ask for a job to the time he picked up a shovel to clean the barns or throw his saddle on a horse.

This particular man's name has escaped my memory, but it could have been John, Dave, or maybe Bob. Bob appeared shifty and soon started altercations with the cowboys. Barn boys qualified for the low end of the totem pole and altercations with wranglers were not a good idea. This Bob character got into deeper and deeper manure. However, Bob managed to hang on until Joe assigned him the job of preparing the campground for the overnight camp-out. Guests gathered at the lodge to learn how to roll their bedrolls with necessary personal items tucked inside. The bedrolls were transported by truck to the camp-out area, while guests mounted their horses Thursday afternoon for a three-hour ride to camp. Bob, along with another barn boy, was to deliver the bedrolls, pile up wood for the fire, and help the cook set up his equipment. The barn boys did not have the privilege to stay overnight, but needed to return to the ranch to shovel the day's manure.

Bob was in a sour mood and smarted off to Joe. "I don't need to shovel all day, this is sh…!" He complained. "Old man, you got it in for me, huh?"

Joe fired Bob on the spot. "Beings you don't like it, you can just pick up your paycheck." With Bob's check signed, Joe escorted Bob to his bunkhouse to gather bedding. The last Joe saw of Bob was when he drove his old junk car through the gate toward Woodland Park.

Joe and the wranglers were too busy that day for the camp out to think much about Bob or why he had been in such a nasty mood or why he was fired. They were glad to be rid of the big mouth troublemaker.

The happy campout ride started that afternoon on a logging road past dark emerald stands of spruce and pine, and clumps of quaking aspen drenched in sunlight. Boulders the size of trucks and houses squatted on lush meadows painted with blue, yellow and red alpine flowers. In that kind of environment, everyone felt happy. Dudes from Chicago, New York and Los Angeles admired the post card beauty, and now and then laughter carried from the trail into the forest of pine and aspen.

Everyone relaxed on mounts they had learned to ride on Monday, even the wranglers were lazily strolling along when the peaceful existence abruptly shattered by a gunshot over the heads of the riders. Another gunshot followed, and slammed into a tree next to Joe. Ping! And again. Ping! There was no drill on how to evacuate dudes under gunfire, and Joe had a bad feeling that someone gunned for him. The instantly alert cowboys moved about as fast as greased pigs, flew off their horses and hustled the dudes off their horses. "Get down, down," they shouted, as they scrambled behind bushes and trees. Miraculously, none of the horses ran off. When no shots followed those first ones, the dudes were rushed off, leading horses away from the battlefield. Joe, always ready with a gun, pulled the rifle from his saddle scabbard and along with three wranglers, remained behind to check out the situation. Once the dudes were out of sight, the cowboys hid behind rocks and Joe shot back from where he thought the shots originated.

The shots were returned in the direction of the cowboys behind their rock. With four cowboys, the mysterious assailant must have thought it wiser to leave the country. He sprinted through the forest toward the main road. The cowboys spotted the running figure darting between trees and boulders and were in hot pursuit while trying to stay out of the gunman's sight. They thought they could beat him down the mountain, by now guessing that the shooter headed for the highway. They also guessed the gunman was shifty Bob. Each cowboy seemed more intent on earning hero status than saving his hide.

The wranglers and Joe correctly guessed that shifty Bob would try to escape to the highway and to his parked vehicle. As he raced for the safety of his getaway car, the wrangler's adrenaline pumped into high gear, and before shifty Bob could start his car, the tire flattened with a well-aimed bullet. Shifty Bob, by now frantic, leaped from his car into the middle of the road where a tourist braked his car in confused surprise. Shifty Bob tried to point the gun at the surprised driver to highjack his car, but the wranglers rushed at shifty Bob. Old West justice followed and a citizen's arrest accomplished with a happy Sheriff taking shifty Bob into custody. As it turned out, shifty Bob was a wanted man by the FBI in another state.

After the shifty Bob incident, wild cowboy tales about shoot-outs and heroic deeds circulated for the rest of the summer and the cowboys puffed themselves up into heroes reminiscent of a successful gunslinger in Dodge City.

"He shot right at me. Could've hit me."

"Man, he was wanted by the FBI. He wouldn't have cared if he killed all of us."

"Remember that rifle he had?"

"Heck, we got him anyways. He was scared."

"Remember when…?" On and on the stories spun into a legend of the shoot-out.

The next shoot out played out toward a less dramatic ending during another summer season at Paradise Ranch. The mystery began in June and ended in September. It was my turn to carry a gun to solve the mystery of the phantom of the cabins. Each morning the housekeeping girls walked to the cabins to clean them if they were occupied or to dust and air the ones waiting for guests. The cabins dotted the fringes of a spruce and aspen forest beyond a horseshoe shaped meadow. At first, stories about a messed up empty cabin seemed nothing more than a maid being forgetful or sloppy, but the girls insisted the cabin had been in perfect order, and in the morning they found a bed indented, a matchbook used, or a sink dirtied. Soon the girls were too spooked to walk alone into an unoccupied cabin.

"There's somebody up there, honestly. I'm not going in there," the maids complained.

I was elected to accompany the maids each morning to check out the situation. Morning after morning, week after week, we checked the cabins that were empty, but never found an intruder. We discovered plenty of signs of a mysterious night caller. My dreams also matched those of the cowboys who fancied themselves as a Wild West hero capturing the bad man. I wanted to catch the bad man and sneaked to the cabins, yanked the door open and pointed my revolver at no one. To my disappointment and somewhat to my relief, I never found an intruder. As time passed, every cowboy including cowgirl hoped to capture the phantom of the cabins. Thus the summer passed, with no progress toward solving the mystery.

The opportunity finally arrived. On a late summer evening, after one of the last rodeos, the cowboys and guests gathered in the Lodge to listen to music and imbibe in refreshments. As the evening wore on and the roof of night descended on the ranch, we visited with guests, danced, drank a few beers, and glanced out of the large picture windows framing the view of the cabins. The moonlit meadow stretched toward the darkness of the forest as we glanced toward the cabins, speculating about the phantom. Suddenly one of the cowboys pointed out a figure running along the fringes of the meadow tinged in white moonlight. We stared for only a heart beat before we bolted from our chairs and raced to the pickups. We were all tuned into the same thoughts. The phantom of the cabins!

"Get your guns, boys", Joe shouted, "let's go".

I jumped into Joe's pickup; removing guns from the gun rack. Several other cowboys scrambled to snatch their guns and joined us in other pickups. We raced toward the cabins, our adrenaline pumping like a geyser. Upon reaching the cabin, the mysterious stranger was nowhere in sight. We figured as much. He would have heard the pickups and fled into the night and we reasoned that the phantom was not an apparition or a figment of the imagination. Joe decided a night patrol might yield results. The cowboys were again after glory, allowing their imagination to roam about capturing a wild man, or a deranged criminal, a prison escapee, or better yet, a serial killer wanted by the FBI. They imagined that the phantom might be a crazed pervert trying to play a hide and seek game. The hunt started in the darkness of the forest, with only patches of moonlight playing hopscotch through the trees. The cowboys dispersed in the woods, guns at the ready. An abandoned water shed received ample warning to "Come out with your hands up", but no one answered before it was pumped full of holes. Zing, ping, ping, the shots reverberated in the empty forest, accompanied by a disappointed, "He ain't in there."

One of the cowboys, a distance from us and deeper in the forest, hollered, "Stop," followed by several shots. We stumbled and ran toward the sounds in the dark but by the time we arrived, the cowboy greeted us without a prisoner. He swore religiously that he had seen a huge figure running behind the dark trees. "By god, that was one hell of a big fella, but he disappeared past them trees. Yelled at him. Warned him to stop or I'll shoot. But he clean got away." We wondered if the cowboy had illusions of grandeur.

We never did know that night if the chase had been part of our active imagination and if the fleeing figure had simply been wishful thinking and did not know additional information until the following Sunday after the rodeo. The rodeo cowboys and girls gathered on the front veranda of the lodge, rehashing the afternoon rodeo and mingling with dudes. Everyone was dusty, spurs jingled, the edge of excitement still alive as wranglers, contestants and guests downed cold beer. Several strangers, apparently rodeo spectators, also lounged on the veranda, and happened to be overheard by a Paradise cowboy as they talked of a shooting the past week. The strangers laughed and talked about their friend being shot in the leg while trying to run from a bunch of crazed cowboys. None of the cowboys confronted the strangers since everyone thought that perhaps the gunfight might not have been a legal activity. We did figure that the fleeing man that night in the forest was no figment of the imagination. We also figured this was our phantom, and since none of the cabins were violated after the nighttime manhunt, we decided the stranger with a bullet in the leg was indeed the phantom of the cabins. The phantom never returned, nor did we ever find out who he was, and the summer of seventy-three ended with wild tales of brave cowboys and an unsolved mystery.

Cussin, ridin', drivin' anything with four legs

Aside from Wild West adventures, horses played the starring role on our patch of the Wild West.

The wranglers of Paradise Ranch, myself included, developed a certain affection or disdain for horses in the dude string. Since the horses that behaved well enough not to kill someone were reserved for the dudes, the wranglers ended up with a string of horses bestowed with innumerable undesirable habits. Some wranglers inherited horses with no discernible bad habits but were simply too much for most dudes to ride safely unless the dude was an expert rider. Sometimes even good dude horses needed a tune up because they developed undesirable habits from dudes who did not understand horses and yanked, pulled, or otherwise spoiled a horse.

The rules were of course always skewed toward the safety of the guest, and wranglers rode anything on four legs assigned to him or her. Joe assigned horses to his cowboy and girl crew on the basis of which horse needed the most riding or which cowboy needed a bit of comeuppance from his holy status that guests tended to bestow on a cowboy. To a guest of course, any cowboy was a hero with a halo around his grimy cowboy hat. Dudes did not know some cowboys were late model cowboys, with no real ranch and rough riding history. For horses, anyone on their back was fair game.

Late Saturday afternoon, the rules of guests riding the good horses and wranglers riding rejects did not apply. The wildest event at Paradise Ranch happened after guests returned from their afternoon ride. All wranglers including yours truly, placed this event at the top of their list of weekly thrills. For the young single cowboys, it probably surpassed clandestine dates with a Chicago blond, or getting away with a rousing drunk, or riding a bucking horse. With no rules, each wrangler picked his favorite mount, the one he thought would bring him home alive. Claims to certain horses were established soon after that first chase. Wranglers awakened quicker than a sleeping coyote getting shot at to the fact that the chase down the mountain was serious business. They learned that with the wrong horse, they could end up in a heap of trouble or in a heap on the ground or plastered against a tree.

The chosen horses had better own excellent breaks, zero to sixty acceleration, and true sports car handling. Surefootedness was an absolute necessity to keep from being maimed or killed. After the chase, wranglers learned to choose mounts and jealously guarded their choice for the Saturday afternoon event.

The event was the bucking horse roundup from the top of Rampard Range plunging over two thousand feet to the valley below. Forty bucking horses from Harry Vold's rodeo stock spent their summer vacation at Paradise Ranch to recuperate from rigorous road trips to rodeos. The bucking horses continued to hone their skills bucking at the weekly Paradise rodeo, but during the week they ran free and wild on the mountain and grew the wild hairs that you want in a good bucking horse. Because of this agreement with Harry Vold, Paradise rodeo was lucky to buck such famous horses as Red Gold, the national bucking horse champion and other fine bucking horses who starred at Calgary, the National Western Stock Show and National Finals Rodeo. Running wild for most of the summer regenerated many a road weary horse.

The bucking horses showed no intention of leaving their Garden of Eden atop the mountain. The chase down the mountain was always in favor of the bucking horses. Wrangler reputations were at stake to bring the horses to the ranch without too many detours, but the bucking broncs did not have a rider to carry and were less hampered. They relished the wild race, leaping over boulders, zigzagging through trees, ducking under low branches, plunging down vertical inclines and over arroyos until they stretched out at the bottom of the mountain for the final heat to the corral with a last desperate attempt at a one-eighty turn to escape back to the mountain.

The broncs enjoyed the race for the love of running, racing each other free and wild and gambling they could outrun the dumb and tame saddle horses. The broncs matched their wits with the tamed horses hampered by the weight of their riders. They were a sneaky bunch, flying into surprise turns here and there, playing a cat and mouse game at a dead run.

I chose my tiny quarter horse mare, Sweet Pea, because she had a wild streak that emerged if she were given half a chance. Most important, I chose her because her breaks worked and she was as sure-footed as a mountain goat. Aside from Sweet Pea, there were plenty of good horses for the mountain chase.

Reginald van Zitt too had chosen a well-behaved horse, adequate for the chase, but Reginald decided he needed to trade to a larger and faster horse. He chose a dapple-gray horse I broke and trained the previous winter. The dapple was handsome, stout, tall and could easily carry Reginald's bony frame covered by little more than a shadow of meat. We named the horse Gray when he first arrived at Paradise as an unbroken three-year-old, and he seemed to have the temperament to carry dudes on precarious mountain trails. Dudes rode Gray on slow rides where everyone rides single file. The guests did not know the reason we never used Gray fast rides. His brakes were deficient and his mouth made of tempered steel. Since we used lightweight curved bits for the dudes to spare the horses any hardship by constant yanking on the reins, the bits were not overly effective. Gray grabbed most of the bits that were put in his mouth and headed his merry way if someone allowed him to shift into fourth or fifth gear. A few cleverly designed bits worked adequately for medium speeds, but in overdrive, Gray could be slowed or stopped with only one special bit.

I promptly and kindly recommended that bit to Reginald.

"Do yourself a favor and use my bit."

"Don't you worry, this one's just fine."

"You'll be sorry." I reminded Reginald…

Reginald figured I was just a girl and he was a man and he could manage any horse in any situation and why would he need the help of a girl's special bit? Accepting the bit would have been a bit like admitting that he needed a pacifier or a seatbelt on the saddle. Reginald used his everyday bit. I reminded Reginald again that Gray had a mouth of steel, but Reginalds flashed a condescending smile. What does a girl know? "Don't you worry none, Miss Freia, we'll get along just fine with this bit."

"Okey, dokey," I answered the man who thought he could handle anything with four hairy legs.

We gathered at the top of the mountain for our usual strategy meeting, each wrangler assigned a position to head the horses down hill. The bucking horses eyed us suspiciously with that knowing glint of mischief. In fine spirits after running wild for a week, they wound up like a drag racer ready for the big heat. You could almost hear them revving up, vroom, vroom, vroom. One batch of horses flew straight down the mountain while another batch veered off to the left. I stayed in hot pursuit on their left flank to turn them eventually back toward the others. The main batch headed straight down the mountain that ended over a cliff precipitously plummeting to a road below. The horses knew about the cliff, but planned to wait until the last minute to dig in their heels and change direction. They loved that kind of chicken game.

The wranglers also anticipated the cliff and reined in their horses in plenty of time to avoid the precipitous drop of twenty feet. Every horse flew around the edge of the cliff. Every horse except Gray. Gray, in hot pursuit of the bucking horses, did not pay attention to Reginald who also knew about the cliff. Gray had been doing a fine job tailgating the bucking horses as long as he didn't need to apply brakes. He thundered on with too much speed to turn and continued to head toward the cliff. Reginald's choices by now were down to two options, neither desirable. He could bail off, or he could hold on to the horn and stick with the gray horse. Reginald decided that bailing off was about as much fun as jumping off a runaway freight train with boulders and trees in the way, so he closed his eyes, gritted his teeth and this ungodly man who never went to church, prayed that Gray would manage the cliff without killing both of them. Gray did manage the cliff jump. He landed on his feet on the road below and, dazed and shocked, used his forgotten brakes and stopped. Reginald was shook enough that he forgot about the rest of the chase. Since the other wranglers continued in hot pursuit toward the corrals, Reginald had to fend for himself. He arrived at the ranch with a headache and with a rather subdued horse with sore legs. He never rode the gray horse again. Reginald did not say anything about the cliff incident and I never said a word about the bit. No need for further comments.

Buddy Harris also had his favorite horse for the chase and for the rodeo event. Buddy had been a fixture at the ranch for several seasons. He'd leave at the end of summer, and then promptly come back like a returning boomerang. One year he hung around wintertime and worked at odd jobs in Woodland Park and helped out at the ranch when an extra hand was needed for cutting wood, repairing saddles and coaches, or mending corrals. In the spring, he brought his bedroll back to the bunkhouse. His revolving status allowed him the privilege of choosing some of the better horses.

Buddy was a good humor man. His curly hair crept out from under his grubby hat, his grin crooked and perpetual. He could always come up with the humorous side of a bad situation. During rodeo time, he worked the bucking chutes until promoted to the announcer position. For the grand entry, every ranch cowboy participated and when Stars and Stripes played on the scratchy record player, it signaled the beginning of the grand entry. We wranglers paired up, winding up like a slingshot to enter the arena at a dead run. Once in the arena, each pair split for a run left and right, circle the arena once, then pair up again for a sliding stop to line up for the National Anthem. After the National Anthem the wranglers split again left and right, pair up at the end of the arena and charged in pairs toward the alleyway leading out of the arena. Since I carried the largest American Flag, I was first to leave the arena, and the rest of the wranglers followed in a dead heat, charging through the alley to clear the narrow passage for the other riders before pulling their horse to a stop. Buddy followed as the last rider and did not have to worry about a rear end collision. He decided stop in the alley.

That day Buddy rode pretty Molly Brown. Molly Brown was a striking mare with a coat the color of bittersweet chocolate, a white blaze and four white stockings. Her conformation was quality quarter horse throughout, but her beauty inside surpassed her outside. She loved everyone and behaved with the perfect manners of a Lady. Everyone loved Molly Brown. She easily captured the hearts of wranglers and guests alike.

When Buddy reined her to a stop from his dead run, she stumbled in a maneuver that she usually performed effortlessly and within the twinkling of a horse's eye, she hit the dirt, front end first, flipping over and landed on her back. Buddy catapulted from the saddle and slammed into the side railing of the alley.

Within moments of the disaster, wranglers raced to the rescue. However, they did not race toward Buddy, they raced toward Molly Brown and left Buddy crumpled in a heap by the fence, dazed with his hat missing. Molly Brown remained upside down, but after the initial shock, she stirred, found her legs under her and heaved herself upright. Everyone breathed a sigh of relief, checked out her legs and consoled her by petting and stroking her neck and rubbing her ears, with cowboy talk reserved for a favorite horse. Buddy found his legs under him as well and found his hat. "Hey, fellas, I think I'm ok,"

"Yea, Buddy, we could see that." The wranglers answered, still fussing over Molly Brown.

"Thanks for the help." Buddy cynically thanked Molly Brown's rescue squad for being so thoughtful about his condition.

Aside from the expected excitement of a rodeo, we also encountered moments of terror and breath-holding episodes. The bull-riding event was the most popular and the floppy eared, gray Brahmans with tremendous bulk entertained guests and cowboys with cantankerous behavior. Other bulls of mixed blood and the devilish looking Brangus with their black hide gave the Brahmans a run for applause. One particular black Brangus-Brahman bull had an affinity for jumping. On any rodeo Sunday when he bucked out of the chute, he attempted to jump the fence, but found himself lurching into posts and railing instead, causing a number of rail birds to scramble for safety.

On one fateful Sunday afternoon, the black bull succeeded in jumping the six-foot fence enclosing the rodeo arena. He did not have any trouble with his getaway, since spectators on the other side of the fence politely made way for the bull. We were all a bit dumbfounded, since we had watched many botched attempts before, but thought that no bull could ever jump that fence successfully. Before the rodeo crew could think about a plan of action, the bull was well on the way in his escape efforts. By now he tasted freedom and he must have figured that if he made it over the rodeo fence, anything else like barb wire or backyard fences were a piece of cake. He plowed through barbwire fences as if they did not exist; he rolled along dirt roads like a freight train. The sleepy mountain community certainly had not expected over a ton of black hair and snot steaming past homes and over yards. When backyard obstacles got in his way, he just mowed down the tiny obstacles, erased a couple of laundry lines and terrified children and adults. Homeowners in Woodland Park had never before had to deal with a ton of flying hoofs, slinging snot from his inflated nostrils. By the time a group of cowboys attempted to follow in hot pursuit, the bull had managed to terrorize the town folks and headed for the peaceful wilderness of the Rampard Range.

His goal appeared to be the wild spaces of the mountains. Because few cowboys could be spared during the rodeo to find the bull, he managed a decent head start. At first the bull was easy to follow because of the destruction and angry people he left in his wake, ready to sue the ranch.

"He charged that away" folks yelled to the cowboys with flopping chaps and horses breathing hard from the chase. "The ranch better pay for my fence."

Late that Sunday, the cowboys found the bull sauntering along a mountain road, his great bulk swinging left and right. He seemed in a hurry after he had left the town and its annoying obstacles behind. When the cowboys found the bull, he naturally had no intention of returning home. No amount of persuasion could change his mind. The best cowboy threats were ineffective. He stared at the dumb cowboys with utter contempt as they shouted, slapped their chaps, swung ropes and cracked bullwhips. He seemed to say quite effectively, "Why don't you little boys just go home." None of the cowboys considered roping a ton of irate flesh with snot flying while shaking his enormous head in anger. Driving him back resulted in increasing the bull's anger. He pawed the ground and challenged any cowboy dumb enough to try anything, but the cowboys were sufficiently intimidated. The trick was not to rope the bull, but how to get him four or five miles back to the ranch. Perhaps when he missed his nightly feed, he'd return willingly. The unanimous decision that Sunday was to do nothing and wait until the next day. The cowboys left the bull without a satisfactory solution. That evening, Joe led the planning session on how to get the bull back to the ranch. Lots of beer accompanied the session to improve thinking.

"We'll try and drive him home first," Joe said.

"That fella might be hungry, there ain't much feed on that road." Buddy added with more hope than reality.

"Maybe it ain't gonna work." Tom expressed doubt about driving the bull home.

"Than here's how we'll try it, boys" Joe suggested. "Me and Buddy will rope him. Reggie and Tom, you can take our ropes and run them to the front and around to the outside of the stock truck, then we get behind while you guys pull." Everyone thought that was a fine idea. The beer probably helped it sound fine.

The next day the Paradise cowboys again attempted to drive the bull along the mountain road, but the bull had not changed his mind and was determined to saunter only where he wanted to saunter. He met any attempts at changing his mind or his direction with snorts, head tossing, pawing and occasional charging when the cowboys became too annoying. Plan B included the stock truck, brought back after conceding that the bull would never change his mind or cooperate. We also had to consider that any successful drive back to the ranch led right back through town where those folks with broken fences and torn laundry lines were still angry. A number of unhappy property owners had already demanded that Paradise Ranch donate money to fix the damage.

The stock truck seemed a good number two idea, but the cowboys and Joe had forgotten there were no chutes or gates to run the bull into the truck. He would have to walk up the ramp like a good little puppy. After a considerable time thinking about last night's strategies, Buddy and Joe roped the bull despite much trepidation. The cowboys were lucky that the bull was a bit tired by now and not as enthusiastic about fighting back. After a respectable time spent coaxing and hoping, the cowboys tied the ropes to the inside of the truck and back toward the rear. The plan was to ratchet him over the ramp inside the truck. Again, the cowboys learned all too quickly that a ton of bull was not easy to ratchet up any ramp into any truck. In fact, the idea proved impossible. Everyone stood around, feeling useless, with the bull occasionally snapping and yanking the rope to show who was boss.

Plan C had become the last strategy on the list of options. Plan C was to pull the bull to his old home with the truck. Everyone agreed unanimously since there were no other ideas and no one wanted to admit they failed to budge this creature. Joe and Buddy tied the bull to the tailgate and Joe elected to drive the truck while the wranglers were to encourage the bull to follow. At least one part of Plan C seemed encouraging. The truck weighed more than the bull.

Slowly, with the truck in low gear, Joe inched home. The bull thought that if he attacked the thing that tried to move him, the thing would be intimidated and leave him alone. He smacked his tremendous bulk into the truck and smashed a taillight. The tail lens cracked, the truck shook from a dull thump the bull delivered with his head. When he found out that the big thing couldn't be scared off, he dug in his heels. That failed to work. The thing still pulled him and started to win the struggle. The truck continued to pull until the bull lost balance and fell on his heaving black side. The cowboys tried to cajole, scare, and encourage the bull to get up. Nothing worked. The bull stubbornly remained on his side and was pulled a few yards. When the bull finally conceded defeat and righted himself, he repeated the sequence. Charge into the truck, knock what was left out of the tail assembly and dent or break something else, dig in heels, throw himself, get dragged in the dirt and gravel, heave upright and get even madder. The bull bellowed a throaty protest, while the cowboys whistled, yelling, "git up, git" and thumped their ropes on their chaps to encourage forward movement. Each time, the truck won by a few yards. After a three or four hours, the bull finally arrived at Paradise Ranch in a rather sorrowful a state of disrepair. His hide received a fair number of scrapes and his pride was no doubt damaged, but the bull must have heeded the lesson. He recuperated in the bull pasture and never again jumped the fence during a rodeo. He seemed content, even if begrudgingly, to curb his wanderlust.

If the bull riding was not thrilling enough, the chariot races were the cliffhanger of the rodeo. Old man Snell accumulated an extensive collection of horse drawn vehicles, and two chariots were the piece de resistance. Rumors had it that the old man bought the chariots from the original Ben Hur movie collection. The rumor might have been true since old man Snell had connections in Hollywood, just as he seemed to have connections in lots of high places. The golden chariots were decorated a la Roman era with knifes protruding from the wheel hubs. Sensibly, the knives were carved of wood.

Although the chariot drivers refused to wear Roman garb consisting of skimpy skirts, they did concede to a flowing cape. The chariots, like all the other horse drawn coaches, had been restored and polished to mint condition. Each chariot was rigged for four horses abreast. Qualities highly prized for chariot racing included a streak of craziness, lots of heart and recklessness and more brawn than brain to dash at Indi 500 speeds, sometimes resulting in a horse unable to keep his legs under him. The rodeo arena had been designed with chariot and wagon racing in mind. The extra large arena encouraged dangerous speeds. To prevent turnovers, the chariots were built with a wide wheelbase and large wheels, sliding sideways in a cloud of dust while the horses steamed ahead with one team as crazy as the other. The crazed horses wound up to frightening speeds and most of the Paradise cowboys either were not allowed to race the chariots or had little enthusiasm to get involved in this hair raising stunt.

During race time, the wives or girlfriends were expected to be stoic, show a measure of faith or if need be, fake enthusiasm that the cowboys would finish the race without ending up in the hospital or a casket, nothing new for a cowboy's wife. She often needed that sort of bravery on any given day. Each Rodeo day, I envisioned Joe catapulted, thrown, dragged or run over. The spectators also expected a good catastrophe.

Shortly before the event, two wild and wooly teams of four abreast were harnessed to their chariots. Joe usually drove one chariot and another cowboy with skill and sufficient craziness or a low IQ drove the other chariot. The ground crew consisted of hefty cowboys and barn boys who hung on to the wild eyed, long legged beasts. As soon as the teams were harnessed, the horses foamed at the mouth, worked up a sweat, and revved up like jet propulsion dragster. When the cowboys let go of the bridles, the horses were off as if shot from a catapult. The races were for real, never staged. Joe and the other cowboy, often Reginald von Zitt who lacked common sense, were in dead serious competition, and the team wasn't about to slow until their lungs gave out, a team crashed or the chariot turned over, whichever came first. The chariot drivers had to keep them under minor control to wind around the turns without hitting the fence or running over each other. Slowing a team was not an option, and any mistakes instantly turned into a catastrophe.

Each season, a certain number of accidents beckoned spectators from the city with expectations to see another 'good one'. Each rodeo season could claim at least one spectacular event. Racing too close to the fence, catching a wheel and flipping the chariot marked one season. One of the horses in the team falling tended to be the most common accident.

Lanky Reginald von Zitt was about to round a corner in the second heat, when one of his horses fell. The horses were wound up like a rubber band and the three upright horses were unable to make their brain function to stop. The horse on the ground did slow them down regardless of their wild-eyed attempt to keep charging forward. Along with a horse on the ground, the wagon tongue started to jam into the ground, threatening to send Reginald catapulting through space. Reginald showed a rare case of quick thinking as he leaped out of his chariot, over one of the horse's backs, jumped to the ground and started running almost as fast as the horses, at the same time hauling on the outside horse's bridle when his boots hit the dirt. The time frame for this transpiration lasted about as long as long as it takes cowboys to say D?@!%#!

Reginald ended up on his feet, stopped the team with several cowboys who ran to the rescue as fast as they could in their high heeled cowboy boots. Whether Reginald intended to save his own hide or the horse's hide is not clear, but intentions aside, he became a hero who deserved plenty of free beer after the rodeo. Spectators at first thought the feat had been planned for the show, in any event, they drove home thinking that they got their money's worth. As a cowboy's wife, I had to admit I felt thankful that Reginald instead of Joe wrecked.

As the summer season waned, and fall blustered into the heart of the Rockies with its glorious burst of colors, Rodeo season ended. The horses sensed the change, the rodeo stock knew and all creatures seemed to recognize that the burden of carrying dudes or bucking their heart out ended for the year. Brisk mornings announced the end of the season. Spiders set forth on their journey on gossamer wings and the first snow sugar coated Pikes Peak. Horses were hauled away to far off mountain pastures and only a few favorites remained at the home corral. Bucking stock returned to Harry Vold's prairie home. Cowboys packed their meager belongings and slung their saddles over one shoulder to drift to Arizona dude ranches or cattle ranches in Nevada. Employees winterized cabins and guestrooms, drain the water and throw white sheets like a hundred ghosts over furniture. The kitchen stood like an aluminum giant, lifeless in its glacial chill. Pace at the ranch crawled to a leisurely stride. Time was set aside for pleasure rides without having to worry about guests falling off their mounts. Joe groomed the dirt in the rodeo arena for the last time and the announcer stand stood like a silent sentry, watching over the big empty arena. The cheers, the scratchy rendition of the National Anthem, the dust and the thrills were dormant for the year. The sentry could sleep.

Fall was also a time to sell whatever horses were found unsuitable for the dude string, were too old, lame, or refused to temper their mean streaks. They were packed into stock trucks and hauled to auctions and we set our sights to a new batch of horses the following spring.

After the usual summer, three or four dozen horses needed replacing for the following summer. Sometimes a deal too good to be passed up happened during the winter and a horse or two was acquired long before the summer season.

Such a deal occurred during late fall when a lone man, whose name is now forgotten, rode into Woodland Park. The newspaper thought him interesting although he did not make the front page. He was unshaven and tired when he rode into Woodland Park. He claimed he rode his pony from the Washington State and now he was broke, hungry and ready to head home via bus instead of pony. He didn't want to work for his bus ticket, he just wanted to sell the pony and figured he would sweeten the deal by throwing in his saddle, bridle, saddlebags, halter and horse blanket. No one in Woodland Park wanted an additional horse to feed during the winter season. Locals suggested that the foreman at Paradise Ranch. One more horse at Paradise ranch made no difference. "Joe Hooper'll buy your paint pony," they said. "Hell, he'll buy anything." They contacted Joe and he decided that he had nothing to lose to look at the pony and saddle deal. The tired man had left the pony in the rodeo arena. The horse looked like nothing special, but appeared to be a solid, everyday ordinary paint horse with good teeth, and cooperated when being handled. Joe figured perhaps he would make a good dude horse or if the deal was sweet enough, he could buy the horse for himself and then sell it for a profit. Joe smelled the profit when he looked over the gear thrown in on the bargain. Also nothing special, but one could always sell a saddle and bridle for a few bucks. Just then, Joe noticed a beautiful 1892 Winchester 25-20 rifle. He zeroed in on his target and started dealing over the horse, calculating if everything was sold separately at a future date, he could double his investment, especially if the rifle was thrown into the deal. Why would the man need a rifle when he headed home on a Greyhound bus?

"Well, I suppose I can use the little horse. But she needs some feed in her." Joe started his horse trading pitch.

"She's a fine horse, tough as nails. Look how far I rode her." The man matched the horse trading pitch.

"We got plenty of horses, need no more, but you did say you were gonna to throw in the saddle and tack?"

"As I said." The man agreed.

"Well, I really don't need a horse or tack, but maybe, if you threw in that rifle…" Joe waited. He really wanted the rifle.

"Well…" The man thought about the deal, still reluctant.

"Beings I don't need another horse I'd be willing to take her off your hands, that rifle would make the deal worthwhile." Joe waited. He knew the man wanted to get home in the worst way and his horse slowed him down.

"Ok, mister, it's a deal."

The hungry fellow tasted the cash already, and he agreed to one hundred and twenty five dollars for the entire lot, including the Winchester.

The bargain was sealed with a handshake and cash, and Joe headed home to return with the stock truck to load the horse. The lucky or perhaps unlucky fellow hightailed it to the bus station, never to be seen again.

The troubles started soon thereafter. Joe announced that we were going to make some money and he was bringing home a horse, tack and a rifle. "The rifle alone is worth more than the horse," he said with a measure of pride.

He drove the stock truck to Woodland Park to load the little paint and bring her home to Paradise Ranch. She loaded just fine after a few minutes of coaxing. So far, all seemed dandy and well. He heard a few smacks on the truck bed, but horses often stomped when they were hauled. Joe started the two-mile drive back to the ranch, when the truck bumped and bounced. Something didn't seem right back there. He stopped to check out the commotion and found an empty truck with a horse walking down the road. Miraculously unharmed, the little paint had climbed the stock racks and somehow managed to jump out without killing herself. She was not interested in running off; she just seemed to want out of the truck. Joe seldom tied horses in the stock truck, thus never considered tying her up. This time he tied up the little paint, but she created a fuss and tried her best to escape.

Joe finally rode her home because he was afraid that our investment would be hurt in her escape attempts. At home, he penned her up in one of the empty corrals, but she jumped the fence and again, seemed happy to jump something and then graze nearby. Quite willing to be caught, he locked her into a different corral with the same rerun. Joe finally deposited her in a pasture, thinking she might be happier if she had room to run, but she liked the room outside the pasture much better. The escapes continued for days. By now, we figured we might not recoup our money because nobody wants to buy a horse that refuses to haul and stay put. At least, we consoled ourselves, we had the saddle and the tack. The rifle made the deal worth wile even if we had to give away the paint horse. The deal became even better when the Winchester ended up as my new deer gun. Who said being married to a cowboy has no benefits?

The little paint seemed too unreliable to keep as a dude horse with her jumping instincts, and might become a bad role model for the other horses. We
decided we'd sell her as a gentle child's horse, there were just a few minor details
left out of her history. We advertised a pony that needed loving care and asked a
reasonable price.

The first call came from parents who wanted to buy their daughter a small
gentle mount they could trust. The loving parents were drawn to the attractive
paint coat and more likely, the attractive price. They bought the little paint, took
her home in an enclosed horse trailer that was impossible to climb out of. They
turned her loose in a pasture and we waited for the first call to come get her after
she jumped the fence a few times. The little girl fell in love with her immediately,
and gave her hugs, kisses and lots of love. The expected call berating us that we
had sold the family an escape artist never came. In the spring, we met the parents
and the little girl complete with the paint, at a parade. The paint seemed totally
enamored with the little girl, and no one mentioned any fence jumping. We figured that the love of the little girl was what the paint had been looking for all
along. Whether the explanation was realistic or not, we preferred to believe that
love sometimes does conquer all.

Most horse deals at Paradise Ranch were not one-horse-at-a-time deals. They
were deals of half a dozen to two or three dozen horses at a time. Horses were
bought by the truckloads. Six draft horses, twenty or thirty dude horses, or ten
ponies. For the new horses, Paradise ranch must have looked like boot camp. The
new mounts were herded into the round corral, tied up one by one, inspected for
blemishes, sores, and cracked hoofs not noted at the auction, or if ordered from a
broker, the horses were total strangers, inspected hoof to ears. The physical
inspection was test number one. Test number two consisted of being tied up
without throwing a fit. The ones who objected were noted as needing extra help
to stand tied as a docile dude horse. We realized when we bought that many
horses all at once, we were at risk for buying someone's spoiled mount. After a
thorough health and behavioral check, shoeing followed vaccinations on those
horses that were retained. The blacksmith more than earned his pay when he
shod new horses. Plenty of new horses had never learned respect and threw a tantrum. Riding followed all the other tests and tasks. The month before the dude
season was spent ironing out bad habits, gentling mounts that refused to cooperate and eliminating undesirable behaviors. Generally, the low man on the totem
pole was assigned the worst of the spoiled horses and the better cowboys were
assigned to training the promising prospects.

With each batch of new horses, one or two were usually a delightful surprise. Some were fine purebred animals, and some showed great promise as a pickup horse, rope horse, or barrel racing horse. Now and then, a green horse presented an opportunity to train a rodeo or trail horse without someone's prior training mistakes.

Each spring, Joe found one or two horses that he thought were special. "Got a horse for you," he'd announce. "That one might be a real good barrel horse." Sometimes he was right; sometimes he was dead wrong.

I often picked barrel racing prospects for myself out of the new batches. Choosing a horse was like being in a candy store where I could have whatever looked delicious. Although Joe and I owned two horses of our own, we did not need to spend good money on buying our own horses. For the once horse crazy teenager who yearned to be a cowgirl and ride horses for the rest of her life, Paradise became a true equine paradise.

For the girl who once dreamed of living and breathing horses, each day was filled with riding and more riding. I had everything. A handsome cowboy, a life in the stunning Rocky Mountains and all the horses I would want to ride. Summer days were spent as a wrangler on the back of a horse; day in and day out, seven days a week. My saddle was my easy chair. Summers were spent herding dudes, but the rides were far from tedious. Especially the fast rides.

Those fast and wild rides were a plum assigned to favorite wranglers and since I was the foreman's favorite wrangler, I naturally drew the plum riding assignments. Stoney Martin and I teamed up to head the wild ride. The guests who passed a tough test in the arena were allowed to join the fast ride. Before that first fast ride, they did not suspect that the fast ride should be renamed the crazy ride. Chicago and New York guests hankered for wild west riding experiences and flew or drove all that way to ride hard and fast. We tried to oblige with a ride they would never forget. Blissfully ignorant of the torture ahead, the dudes thought we were joking when we informed the small group of guests that this ride would be rougher than the old cowboy movie rides.

"So listen up." Stoney and I started our pre-ride speech. "This ride's wilder than a wild one, you might get hung up in a tree limb, you might part company with your horse once or twice, and you won't have time to catch your breath. Do you still want to go?"

Oblivious, the selected guests agreed to ride with all stops pulled out, along with some valiantly hidden insecurity by the looks on their faces, which belied their affirmative head nodding.

Stoney or I rode lead while the other brought up the rear to pick up the pieces. We warmed up our riders with a controlled run over a flat meadow or a wide road leading toward the steeper, rougher and unforgivable parts of the mountains. Relieved, the riders thought that this was a piece of cake and figured they had it made. With the first test passed, we asked the riders if they were ready for something a little wilder. If they nodded affirmatively, we presented the deal.

"So here's the deal if you want something wilder. If anyone falls off you owe us a six pack. If anyone falls off twice, you owe two six packs. Everybody game, or do you want to quit?"

Some dudes seemed to hide doubt while others set their chin stubbornly. Nobody backed out of the challenge. They figured if they stayed on, they could tell tall tales of how they survived the wildest ride of their life. The agreement was sealed and we were off.

The trail we chose ran under low tree branches, hairpin curves, zigged and zagged around trees and boulders, dips, gullies, along precipitous cliffs, and through arroyos. We insured as much safety as was possible by choosing only the best and most trustworthy mountain horses that manage anything despite a dude's shortcomings. As soon as the wild ride started, we noticed riders suddenly applying a death grip on the horn and self assured smiles were wiped off the previous confident face as the horses whipped around curves, ducked under trees, jumped gullies and flew over steep hills like a chase car in San Francisco. Surprisingly we did not earn as many six packs as expected, although the six pack supply was adequate. When the ride ended, the brave lost their pallor and started bragging about the ride.

In 1975, the wild rides ended.

The glory of the dude ranch days faded into memory. Paradise Ranch had sold several times since old man Snell left and no one managed a financial success. The ranch had been a dream for one last Texas Corporation, but the dream turned into a financial nightmare. The new owners declared bankruptcy and the halcyon days were over.

For Joe and I, life in cowboy Disney land ended. The job search was on. I mourned the best cowboy job in the world; our pine paneled home, our rodeos and our remarkable string of horses. The opulent life became a sweet memory. Sadness weighted heavily, and again, worry knocked on our door. The little crumb-crunchers packed their toys, I packed my china and crystal, and Joe packed his anvil and our saddles. We joined the hundreds of cowboys on the move, seeking dream jobs, greener pastures, shorter hours, kinder bosses, or less drafty homes. We moved into a house in Chrystola Canyon two miles from the ranch and anxiously checked the Western Lifestock Journal for ads. Joe's hopes were dashed week after week with ads that described fence fixing, dairy cows, or showing horses. He complained how nobody wanted a real cowboy anymore, and I worried how to pay for the food and rent.

Joe accepted a job at the mines in Cripple Creek, and worked in the bowels of a mine. He brought in extra money by shoeing horses. I stood in line for food stamps with two little tykes by my side. We anticipated each week that the Livestock Journal would change our lives with one last perfect cowboy job. The hardships and renewed worries were tough to endure after nine glorious years. When a job finally appeared in the want ad column, we moved out of the shadows of Pikes Peak back to cattle ranch country in hot and dry California. The halcyon days were over.

7

Bandannas, Boots and Wheels

The dress code for cowboys is as inflexible as tightly strung barbwire. For cowgirls, it's a bit more relaxed because we all know that women are more flexible and like fashion changes so they can have an excuse to shop. Not so with a real dyed in the wool cowpoke. Try to sell a cowboy who has been wearing 501 Levis a pair of Wranglers or vice versa! Worse yet, try to sell him a pair of Calvin Klein's and you could end up looking down the wrong end of a Colt 45.

Joe wore Levi 501's all of his life. He might have been born in them. Although Wrangler jeans are acceptable as genuine cowboy pants by genuine cowboys with a wad of tobacco in their cheeks, Joe always looked crooked at anybody who wore them. As if they were not real cowboys, or they were gay, or tried to hide something awful, like being born in the city and didn't learn to ride a horse at age three. Cowboys in Wrangler jeans tend to appear less bow legged than their country cousins in Levi-Strauss jeans. I have a sneaky hunch that the Levi's are cut that way because that's how they hang on the laundry line. Bowed. Because the 501 jeans have buttons, Joe considered zippered pants sissy. In Joe's book, real men wear button up jeans. Perhaps zippered cowboys believe that button-up cowboys are the sissy bunch. On the practical side, Joe insisted that button-up jeans last longer because the zippers don't jam. On cowboy salary that is important because jeans have to last at least five years or 500 miles on horseback, whichever comes first. That of course is asking a lot of a pair of pants, therefore the five-year or 500 mile expectation includes iron on patches. During the sixties when bell-bottom pants were the fashion rage, Wrangler designed both straight leg and a bellbottom pant. Even conservative cowboys started wearing bellbottom jeans. Not Joe! The bellbottom jeans were easier to pull over a high topped pair of boots, but for Joe, that was no excuse to wear such an odious piece of clothing. God meant pant legs to be tapered and fit snugly over boots to where sometimes Joe cursed because the top of the boot and the bottom of the 501's were the same circumference, but that small problem wasn't about to change Joe's mind about buying even conservatively bellbottom pants. With a tweak of the imagination, one can guess what Joe thought of cowboys who wore not only other brand jeans but also the kind that flared. Holy mother cows of the range. Those so-called cowboys shouldn't be allowed on a horse's back.

The bellbottom cowboys, in Joe's opinion, wore the comfortable jeans because they could not get on a horse with pant legs that severely restricted knee movement. The pants were like a vice grip, presenting major restrictions when the cowpoke had to get on a horse fast. The idea behind wearing tight pant legs is to prove that getting on a horse that thinks the gate in the Kentucky Derby just opened, is no effort at all.

Come to think of it, wrangler jeans are supposed to fit men with bigger butts according to Joe. He did not talk about this subject in public, but he was quite serious about the butt theory. He felt quite proud of his little butt. It must have been whittled down over all the years sitting in a saddle. He reckoned Levis specifically fit men who had flat and trim real cowboy butts. Whoever said a cowboy is a scientific creature?

The adornment of Levis is also important. The back pocket is the true sign of a he-man. Countless cans of chewing tobacco eventually wear the honorable white ring into the blue cloth. The other back pocket always sprouts a bandanna. Preferably red, but Joe conceded to other colors when I turned adventurous and bought blue and green. The hankie is part of the cowboy get up that I considered disgusting. Joe got it good and used before throwing it into the laundry and by then the cloth was glued together in many spots. I always picked his hankies up rather gingerly, generally accompanied with a wrinkle of the nose, by the edge with two fingernails and threw them into the old wringer washing machine. He used the clean hankies to protect his neck against cold in the winter and to dip into water tanks to wipe down sweat on a hot summer afternoon. The clean hankie never made it to the laundry pile until it was good and glued together from blowing his nose after many dusty rides.

The belt is another adornment on cowboy jeans except on Joe's Levis. He wore no belts and swore he'd never own one. Sometimes he recalled jokes about cowboys with big belt buckles and one can guess at the kind of jokes, but generally, he said not much because most of his friends wore belts with buckles.

The western styled shirt is another item where changes or concessions are out of the question although he accepted that other cowboys wore shirts without a western cut, a yoke sewed onto the front, back and sleeves, snaps instead of buttons and pockets with snaps. The snaps are always an annoying hassle and crushed or tear off shirts when laundered. Wringer washers during my years as a young cowboy wife were voracious beasts that preferred a diet of pearl snaps. When we lived at a feed lot in Eastern Colorado, we inherited an ancient wringer washing machine. Joe immediately recalled nostalgic thoughts about his mother washing his clothes in such a machine. "God, I remember my mom washing in one of those. She was a hard worker, but what a lady!"

I could dredge up no nostalgia since I had to wring the clothing through the rollers instead of watching soap operas while the laundry washed itself. Besides pearl snaps, those rollers tried to eat everything that slipped between its jaws. I finally hit on the useful idea of investing in a handy dandy gadget to install new snaps, buying a dozen snaps at a time from western stores who obviously knew the housewife's dilemma. Ironing around snaps, yokes and trim is time consuming slave labor. The shirts are the abyss of the weekly ironing basket and even with lots of practice, I hated ironing around all that piping, the snaps, and the pockets with flaps and snaps. At least I could watch General Hospital while ironing Joe's time consuming genuine he-man western shirts. Once I bought him a practical shirt with no flaps and snaps but pockets with a single plain button.

"That looks so good on you." I praised in hopes of convincing him to change his tastes.

He flat out stated, "I can't wear a shirt like that." He insisted he might lose his job if he wore 'that' shirt, because he would loose the tally book tucked into the shirt pocket and then he couldn't account for which steers and what numbers were shipped. Back to flaps and snaps.

The shirts, Levis and bandannas were at least affordable. Even in the days when cowboy wear was priced to fit a cowboy budget, ten-X hats and handmade boots ate a hole in the checking account. Not a penny was spared when buying these two items. Joe did not believe in cheaper straw hats. He refused to wear a straw hat even if the scorching sun burned his balding scalp. The hat had to be beaver or nothing at all. I have to admit that the beaver felt hats held water and you could pour water over your head on those hundred degree California days. In a thirst emergency, you could also drink from the hat, but generally, that was not advisable because of sweat contamination. Beaver felt hats also last much longer than straw, somewhere on the average of three to five years. We worked out a system where Joe always owned two hats. Once was dress and immaculate, the other battered and stained with sweat that coated the hatband with a salty crust. The old hat lasted until the dress one started to show signs of wear. At this point, Joe exchanged the dress one for the work one and the meager paycheck would have to bear the cost of a new hat.

The hat could be no less than five to ten X beaver quality and had to be a Stetson. The style had to be the old-fashioned ten-gallon hat and had to be black. There were times when Joe bought a silver belly dress Stetson, but he preferred his hat as black as the bottom of a well at midnight. Joe believed that he would appear too much the good guy in a light colored hat, probably influenced by too many western movies. Nobody messed with Joe when he wore his black Stetson. Nobody. Not event the horse! When we treated ourselves to a beer at the local bar and the night wore on toward the time when tongues loosened, Joe was respectfully left alone. Even in drunken stupor, the men in bars instinctively knew that you never ever bothered a cowboy with a big black hat. Somebody did once, said something offensive and they got too close to Joe with his black hat. The next event found the offending man flying through the swinging doors a la John Wayne movies and resting in the parking lot about twenty feet beyond the punch from the guy in the black hat. I can't prove this hypothesis, but I think one of the reasons Joe always wore black hats is because the big black was the warning for others to watch their step, akin to a gunfighter wearing fancy pearl handled six shooters.

One other reason for wearing a hat in public might have been Joe's ever increasing bald spot and hats covered up the embarrassing spot. Naturally, the hat became a necessity when he tried to impress the Ladies. Of course, Joe would never admit to that sort of reasoning. Lucky for him, in the West, it is not only acceptable but expected that a cowboy will wear his hat when in a bar other indoor establishments, although Joe removed the hat if we ate dinner in an upscale restaurant. With a meager paycheck, that remained a rare event. Breakfasts or lunches at the local greasy spoon did not deserve removal of the hat. Save the vanity and death to anyone who would touch his hat. Touching a hat is as much of a sin as someone touching private parts in public.

My enchantment with black hats lasted only as long as the hat remained new. During the summer, the hat turned into a downright disgusting object. On days when the noon heat blisters the range, the hat turns into a pungent piece of felt with the sweet and sour smell of sweat permeating the entire house. On those days, I never allowed Joe to bring his hat into the house. He had to take it off in the mudroom or on the porch. He complied but never understood what was so unpalatable about his hat.

Boots are the most important and the most expensive item. Boots cost plenty when buying them off the rack but rack-boots were not considered an option. They were hand-made or by gosh he would wear none at all. Joe never owned a pair of shoes or even sneakers in his life. On hot dry Sunday afternoons, when we drove to the beach with the little whippersnappers so they could play in the sand and ocean surf, Joe wore his boots. He will be the one true cowboy to die with his boots on.

I dreaded the year when boots are due. They bit a sizable chunk out of the paycheck, which was never enough anyway. Buying boots is like buying expensive radial tires with fancy design and stitching for a four-wheel drive. The boots had to be handmade-to-order-boots. When we were first married, Blucher boots of Olathe designed boots that you might discover in today's antique shops and are collected by non-cowboys who decorate heir homes with a western flavor. Joe always ordered the most under-slung high heels possible. The tips were reinforced with a fancy overlay wing tip design, double sewed, sometimes scalloped or pinked. The shank had to be steel because a cardboard shank would break down in a day when jammed into an oxbow stirrup. I avoided arguing that only the most superlative quality would do. Boots were not an item to buy; they were an investment, acquired every other or every third year and had to withstand substantial abuse. The tops were always riotously colorful: Green, blue, red, with at least eight rows of a fancy stitched design. There were cutouts of every imaginable design and shape, always a different color than the top. The tops had to be tall enough to rise up just under the knee with a deep scallop and either mule ears or fancy boot loops to pull on a boot, which fit like a surgical glove. When Joe felt like dressing fancy for the day, the boots would be pulled on over the jeans. On dreary workdays, the boots might disappear under the jeans. The price tag for this custom made item is at least half of a monthly paycheck. When Blucher Boot Company went out of business back then, Joe considered it a funeral announcement. The Blucher boot, in Joe's opinion, was the mark of a real cowboy. Bluchers were not just real cowboy boots, but the old guard, the cowboy's cowboy boot. We found other boot companies that jumped on the bandwagon but Joe grumbled about the imitations.

Because of the price tag, boots had to be resoled and resoled and again resoled. Even full soles were expensive enough that I fretted and worried as his soles wore thin. Because of the bowlegged nature of cowboys, the heels never wore even and the boots always fell over when they stood without a man inside of them. Taking them off often required a bootjack or me. I figured he could pull off his boots by himself if he wouldn't wear tight tapered jeans that imprisoned the boot top and prevented considerable knee bending and gymnastics to extract the boot.

In most circumstances, I didn't fancy myself as my husband's maid, but in the case of boots, I made sure they were cleaned of mud and manure, regularly conditioned with mink oil, and if wet, stuffed with newspapers. I didn't volunteer for this lowly job out of kindness but out of concern that the boots might wear out faster and then we would have time to scrimp for a new pair.

Although Joe was vain in an old-fashioned cowboy way, so was I. Tight jeans that looked painted on were part of my vanity wardrobe. For a few years, stretch jeans were the fashion and for the first time, I could get on a horse without bunching the jeans up around my knee so I could bend that left knee to step into the stirrup. When the stretch jeans were the fashion statements, I bought myself a pair of turquoise-silver lame bell-bottoms. They were flashy for barrel racing and I hoped would intimidate other barrel racers. I figured they might secretly believe I was a real hot shot since I dared wear such flashy pants. They also showed off my trim figure because in those days I was thin as an aspen tree.

Joe never begrudged my fancy western clothing. He encouraged me to buy only the best Stetson, and had just as much fun choosing colors and designs for my handmade Blucher or M.L. Leddy boots. Our budged was the sobering factor that dictated limitation on how fancy and how much we indulged. In the early days of marriage, before the little crumb-crunchers, I sewed many of my dress western threads. So did the other cowboy wives and we proudly compared our accomplishment on a budget as thin as dental floss. We knew that our fancy duds were part of the game to entice a cowboy into our web when we were single and than we had to keep up the image of a sharp looking cowgirl after marriage.

The fancy going-to-a-wedding duds were another necessity and an investment that had to last for thirty years. Joe invested in one charcoal gray western suit. We figured that it would be in fashion until he died and then it could serve as the funeral attire. The suit was necessity with numerous weddings after a starry-eyed city girl married a cowboy she had snagged at Paradise Guest Ranch. When Joe wore his charcoal suit with the red vest and the immaculate silver belly dress hat, he was a prize that many a young city girl eyed with longing.

The expense of a saddle was and still is another long-term investment. The investment cost as much as a used car or pickup. A cowboy has to figure on two to three saddles in a lifetime. Of course wearing out a saddle is directly proportionate to its use. Joe's saddles often received daily punishment. It had to withstand a thousand-pound steer or a raging bull yanking on the horn. Daily rope burns marked the leather and horses cared less what happened to the saddle. When in a bad mood they tried to roll on it, scrape it against fence posts, and fall on it to express their defiance. Rain soaked his saddle throughout a wet season, and the heat and dust dried out the leather. Five years after our fateful union, Joe had come to the end of the patch-up possibility. The old rig had lasted twenty years. We re-calculated our meager saving and checking account and ordered a new saddle. He bought the roughest saddle on the western market, cut from rough-out leather, an extra thick grade and a plain-Jane design with no fancy carving or lacing. The horn was beefed up and the hardware could have been used to hoist an elephant. The rough-out leather soon glistened from daily use and the beefed up horn needed further reinforcing with two dozen wraps of inner tube strips. The saddle, we hoped, would last for at least twenty thousand miles of riding or until retirement.

My saddle was still the economy variety that I had purchased at Miller Stockman in Denver during my single days when I had even less to spend and I was double and triple as poor as in our state of married bliss. The economy model at Miller Stockman cost a hundred and ten dollars. It was a pretty saddle with a leaf pattern stitched into the leather and sported a quilted seat. The saddle was usable for barrel racing and trail riding, but did not withstand the torture of roping. After the birth of our first crumb-cruncher, Joe thought I deserved a prize for going through the ordeal of bringing a little cowpoke into this world. "Pick any saddle you want," he boasted "we can afford it. Get the best."

The affordability was a problem I did not confront.

After my first delivery of a healthy little cowpoke, Ralph Shimon delivered my dream saddle. A floral acorn pattern adorned the leather, engraved silver capped the horn and cantle and forks were laced with silver. The saddle was as beautiful as it was tough, rugged enough for roping and withstanding a truck rolling over it. With all the trappings, it weighed forty-five pounds and I weighed ninety-eight pounds. It takes no mathematician to figure out that the saddle weighed as much as half of me, soaking wet. Lifting half of my weight above my head to throw onto the back of a tall horse was a feat I mastered and impressed cowboys who wanted to come to the little damsel's rescue.

Saddle pad and blankets were another ongoing expense and financial headache every two or three years. The pads were soaked with sweat, had to be washed and finally wore to shreds. During the sixties and seventies, we topped each pad with a genuine Navajo blanket, but the eighties brought about a new appreciation for American Indian crafts. The Navajo blanket values soared from twenty dollars to several hundred or even a thousand dollars depending on the uniqueness and quality. Our Navajo's were transferred from the barn to the house and I bought imitation Navajo blankets for the horses. The horses of course never cared one way or the other and the classic Navajo rugs spruced up floors and walls.

The pickup strained the budged even more than boots, hats, saddles and ropes. Our pickup always looked like something that had been hauled out of a mud pile and smacked by a hammer or two by four. Mud clung to the fenders, dents battered the tailgate and scratches decorated the bed, but Coach and Black Puppy considered it their Cinderella coach. They looked forward to a ride in the pickup bed. With our budget, even when pickups were not considered a luxury vehicle, we could never afford a new one. The last pickup we bought lasted about ten years and looked like an old wreck that had never seen one good day. It metamorphosed from a light brown, scratched and dented bed with stained torn seats to an iridescent grasshopper green with striped seat covers and a rebuilt engine with a shiny new hitch for the horse trailer. At least we had come up in the world by owning a fourteen-year-old pickup instead of a 1949 Studebaker. I dressed up the pickup with a new tape deck that blasted a Willie Nelson song through the open window, competing with the rumble out of rusted tail pipes.

"My heroes have always been cowboys
And they still are it seems,
Sadly in search of and one step in back of
Themselves and their slow moving dreams…"

Never mind the dents, the scratches, the rust spots.

8

The Seasons of my Heart

The four seasons of the year entwine intimately with the way of ranching. Life breathes and depends on seasons. Subservience to nature exists for the rancher that is most foreign to the city dweller.

For those who are uninitiated to the magnitude of the seasons on life, the worst challenge may be driving to work on icy roads. Once you mastered that task without ending up in the ditch, the rest of the day is spent in a dry, climate-controlled office. Snow might mean the joy of skiing or sledding, summer sweats mean the air conditioner quit and you have to drive with the window down until you find a parking place at the beach or hibernate in an air conditioned room.

The seasons of my life as a cowboy's wife often announced their presence with punishing hardness. But for each dusty, drenched, or bone chilling day, there were Indian summer days, mild winter afternoons that gently warmed the heart, soothing summer rains, spring bursting into riotous bloom, and a Chinook erasing the mark of winter.

Fall

I have no favorite season. Choosing a season is as difficult as choosing a favorite dessert. Cherry Pie, Strawberries and Cream, Chocolate Mousse? If someone forced me to choose, I might favor fall. Spring, winter and summer are capable of malicious and brutal presentations, but fall is the season to bask in the last warm rays under crystalline skies. It is a time to luxuriate and rejoice in the brilliance of nature, presented regally by every shade of red, yellow, purple, green, amber and gold. It is a time to wind down from summer and prepare for the cold season before winter slaps you harshly in the face.

Fall in Colorado ranch country is synonymous with kicking back, a mellow time after a summer of early-rise mornings, no days off, and the days ending long after sunset. At Paradise Ranch, the last guest caught a plane or train back to Chicago. Cabins were locked, the furniture covered with white sheets to stand like ghosts until the next summer. The wood was chopped for personal use with expectations of a long, snowed in winter. The reasons for riding changed to the sheer joy of sharing time with friends and or riding alone. The trail to the top of Rampard Range mutated into a celebration of fall, surrounded by stillness except for the crunch of freshly fallen leaves under the horse's hoofs, and the hundred hues of metamorphosed leaves. Amber, cadmium yellow, old gold, ochre brown, burnt sienna, fuchsia, burnt umber, titian, and pure gold

Tiny spiders on gossamer wings traveled to unknown destinations, the last of the fall mushrooms poked through layers of composted forest floor, permeated by the aroma of a musty cellar, and the briskness of the air was tempered by the sun's warmth, the last left over rays of summer.

The first snow of the season knocked on the door of the Rockies while fall thought it still owned the mountains. The first snow rarely presented a threat. Instead, the first snow painted a picture of stark contrast between valleys and mountains. Leaves that clung tenaciously to trees continued to paint the lower eight to ten thousand foot in brilliant gold and reds, but Pikes Peak was cloaked in a fresh cap of sugary frosting. Although we lived and breathed this resplendent view from dawn to sunset, we never tired of admiring the exquisite beauty. Inside our snug pine paneled home at Paradise Ranch, a picture window framed Pikes Peak like a post card to impress Easterners. We lived in the postcard that tourists send back home and a 'wish you were here' scribbled on the back.

Fall also marked the beginning of the dude horse's long period of recuperation. A few favorite horses continued to live at the ranch, but the rest of their pals moved to a leased mountain ranch. There they could pretend to be wild horses for the winter and run and hide without the presence of stern wranglers or silly dudes. Shorter days and a weakened sun signaled the time to grow a thick furry coat in preparation of zero degree days and below-zero nights in the shadows of Pikes Peak.

At Rancho San Fernando Rey in Southern California, fall walked in with a heavy foot. Fall refused to bring the relief of the mild Indian summer days in the Rockies. September recorded the hottest days of the year. Temperatures climbed above a hundred, and folks felt their breath snatched away by the intense heat. The hills reeked of scorched dust instead of musty earth and scrubbed pines. The skies during the day were still and lifeless because nothing wanted to fly during the heat of the day. Buzzards looked down on horses, waiting for them to die from heatstroke. Water and shade was the most prized possession. Ten or eleven in the morning finished riding, the cowboys returning to the ranch for a siesta, to tackle more riding and cattle work later in the afternoon. If they rode the back forty, they holed up under sycamore and bay trees in canyons, and slept away the noon hours with their hat firmly planted over their hot faces to ward off pesky flies, the only life form to revel in the heat. While Paradise Ranch horses frolicked on brisk mornings with a breath of frost on the grass, horses at Rancho San Fernando Rey remained coated with salty white sweat, and cowboys complained. "Hell, summer's never gonna end".

There were few places on the ranch where one could find relief from the blast of the mid day sun. Parched grassland was so tinder dry that a pickup's exhaust could spark a fire. Everything, including oak trees, brush, and the cracked dry earth just seemed to quit living, in a dazed state waiting for early fall rains. Eagles hid in the sparse shade of dead trees, deer and pigs holed up in sheltering brush. Everything withered, except the horse flies. Were they sent by the devil? I knew of one secret haven on the ranch where the horseflies were absent, repelled by the pungent odor of ancient bay trees shading a narrow canyon. Shallow pools of cool water nestled between smooth boulders, and the sun couldn't penetrate the massive trees no matter how hard it tried to burn up everything in sight. The canyon was like a secret kingdom and highly prized by the cowboys and even the horses. If the boss could not find a crew anywhere on the ranch, he could win a bet about where they were hiding.

Fall in Southern California was just an extension of summer, with no relief until sometime toward November when a hint of Indian summer breeze attempted to soothe the earth. The real relief did not arrive until the rains of winter.

Winter

Winter on ranches ranged from a magical winter wonderland in the Rockies to an eruption of emerald colors in coastal California to a time when hell froze over. Southern California ranches burst and exploded into a sea of emerald, crazily patched with splashes of brilliant hues. Fields of flaming orange poppies, deep azure lupines and whitewashed daisies dazzled the human eye. Although my favorite season remained fall in the Rockies, I cherished winter in coastal California. The first winter rain washed away the harshness of the parched earth and the hills transformed from brittle yellow, brown and gold to soothing, lush greens. The land metamorphosed into an emerald gem. Life began, as if the earth was created from scratch. The transformation appeared within days of the first rain and seemed more of a miracle than a normal process of nature. The animal's listlessness throughout the long period of relentless heat changed to playfulness. Cows and steers eagerly clipped the young green grass. Calves ran with their tails pointing straight up. Placid horses bucked for the sheer joy of bucking. Colts and fillies chased after nothing in particular. After a rain, the ranch horses reveled in rolling in the muddiest spot in the corrals, particularly just before they were to be ridden.

California horses also grew winter coats, but they were not near as luxuriously wooly as their mountain cousins that transformed into a ball of fluffy fur.

California ranch winters were a time to revitalize and recuperate. And hope. By November, ranchers crossed their fingers and checked the Farmer's Almanac for a good wet year. Winter crops, fat cattle prices and a crop of calves depended on a wet year. Cowboy jobs could depend on a wet year. Everyone hoped for a wet year to survive with a little extra cash in their Levi and Wrangler pockets. During a generous winter, the grass tickled a horse's belly and waved in the wind like a tremendous ocean. Sometimes the rains were gentle, a mist enveloping the verdant hills, transforming the country into a symphony of gently descending water. Some winters the rains viciously attacked the land, rivers swelling and dry riverbeds carving out new arroyos to rearrange banks and shores. The gentle showers changed to growling, rumbling threats. Each day boots had to be scraped free of mud that clung to soles like glue. The boots were stuffed nightly with newspapers to dry them out and keep from shriveling and curling their toes. Joe owned two pair of boots that were alternated to allow one pair to dry. I avoided wearing my fancy J.C. Blucher boots because I knew we could not afford hand-made boots for another year or two. Some of the cowboys wore over-boots in the corrals where mud was ankle deep, mixed with soggy manure. Even the most careless cowboy removed their boots before they entered a house, knowing that the wife would kill him if he brought the mud into the kitchen. "Leave the mud confined to the porch" was a cardinal rule. Often, the seams of the Levi pants were crusted in mud and a wife insisted he take off the pants along with the boots at the end of the day.

In the other world, the one where hell freezes over every winter, mud was usually frozen into bumps and miniature hills. If bugs dared wander into the frozen landscape of a corral, they might have thought they were negotiating the wilds of the Arctic or the mountain ranges of Alaska. The problem of living in frozen hell was keeping your feet from freezing. Regular cowboy boots were killers when you had to get up on a forty-below morning to feed the cattle. At the cattle ranch in Parshall, Joe and I could not wear cowboy boots on those winter days. That was the only time Joe conceded to wearing something besides genuine handmade cowboy boots with under-slung heels. We started with two pair of thermal socks. Felt liners followed to fit into a snowmobile boot. Lots of wiggling room for the toes was a vital for survival. The liners were pulled out of the boots at the end of the day and placed by the heater to dry. Our narrow oxbow stirrups were exchanged for wide bell shaped ones that accommodated a fat snowmobile boot. We never ventured outside early in the morning without bundling up like an overstuffed mummy.

In the morning, before the sun soothed the white world, the air crystallized with ice particles. A whinny or a hawk's whistle shattered the icy air like a crystal glass smacked by an iron rod, and every step crunched and crackled when walking between the barn and the house. A cough or bark sounded as if thrown against brittle glass. When snow fell heavily to mound another foot on top of the last three or six feet, footsteps, horse's neighs or a hawk's call dampened and muted as if packed away in cotton. Nights were unadulterated in stillness, as if no living thing existed while the land locked everything into an icy prison.

Morning after morning, the ice had to be chopped for the horses, the cattle, and the milk cow. Sometimes the waterlines for the house froze and stayed that way for a week or two until the land breathed a sigh of relief from the arctic fronts. "They're froze again." I informed Joe and he just shrugged. "Well, I give up".

I never complained because the frozen pipes seemed less of a problem than hacking away sheets of ice from water tanks and through the creek.

In this miserable glacial mountain valley, I helped feed the cattle on snow blown pastures. Later in the day, we watched the round space heater defrost our car if I wanted to drive into Hot Sulfur Springs or Granby. We never worried about it snowing because there was always snow. Snow on top of snow and more snow on top of the last layer. Until spring, not a single gravel rock peeked through the snow packed on dirt roads. Nobody ventured outside without survival clothing, not even to milk the cow. The bitterness of winter was a constant companion in this lonely Colorado valley.

To survive the endless drain on energy to heat the body, we ate so much fat that we should have been dead from a heart attack by the end of winter. After an hour or two in open mountain pastures with the wind chill at seventy below, our bodies used up tons of calories. I never thought how lucky I was to fry slabs of bacon, sinful thick steaks, and potatoes slathered in bacon fat. The house permeated with steam from the kitchen and the glorious smells of steamed hot chocolate.

Winter on the ranch in Parshall was an exercise in survival. A good chunk of the paycheck was earmarked for survival clothing. Down jackets designed for a Himalayan expedition, insulating wool socks, snowmobile suits and snowmobile boots, gloves with extra insulating fur or wool, real wool sweaters and real wool shirts from Eddie Bauer, thermal underwear, and ski masks to prevent icicles on the face. The dressing part itself in the morning turned into a time consuming ritual.

We were not thrilled about living in a deep freeze, but the dogs and cats were less than happy in their frozen world. By the hangdog look of their faces they thought they were being punished if they were not allowed in the house. Even Coach and Black Puppy were less than enthusiastic about going along on outings to the cow pasture or on a ride to check fences and waterholes in creeks. The dogs and cats hid in the barn if they were not allowed in the house, and came out only when the high altitude sun burned off the top layer of ice on the ground. On the coldest days, they begged relentlessly by the front door and followed us with dejected eyes as if to ask, "you don't love us?" When we felt plenty guilty, we allowed the menagerie into the house. Nights were too dangerously cold. Coach and Black Puppy snuggled into old blankets on the mud porch in the house. The dogs thanked us gratefully with a wag of their stubby tails, but the cats felt far too entitled to show any grateful gestures although they could curl up on the couch.

Winter at Parshall was also a world of beauty. Its starkness often remained devoid of color except for blue and white. On those hellish cold days, the sky changed to a brilliant blue and clouds hung ominously over white mountain peaks, steel blue and gray and dense with ice crystals. When night fell, temperatures dipped further below the below zero temperature of the day, and the land plunged into an abyss of deep purples and blues. During those purple evenings, elk descended from the high plateaus to raid haystacks. As silent as the oncoming night, they moved through pastures and hoped for someone to have forgotten to close the elk fence around the stacks. The next morning, if they sun graced the day, the lonely mountain world transformed back to pale blue and brilliant white. On non-killer days, it was great fun to take the horse out for a run, leaping through new powder snow from the night before.

Horses and cattle hunched against the arctic wind and soaked up high altitude sun during bright clear days. For the horses, there was less work except for our Percheron draft horse. The big wooly fellow had to pull the sled every morning to feed the cattle. He accepted his lot, tediously and methodically tromping through hay meadows while Joe dispersed chunks of hay to hungry cows, anxiously mewing for their breakfast. Since cattle were brought down from high country and gathered around the home pastures in the winter, horses never traveled far from the ranch to check on the herd.

Traveling to the backcountry on horseback would have required snowshoes on horses. Only elk, deer and snowshoe rabbits managed to negotiate the backcountry. On most days, the horses remained in the corrals and home pastures, looking bored and often sleeping the day away.

At Paradise Ranch, horses were also not necessary except for pleasure rides and occasionally checking on the herd of dude horses shipped to far off mountain pastures. Winters at Paradise Ranch were mild and often pleasant compared to Parshall's hell, and livestock could winter in the backcountry sloping away from the worst winter influence of Pikes Peak. After a summer of daily rides, the few horses remaining at the home corrals at Paradise seemed to enjoy the occasional ride to the top of Rampard Range or the yearly outing to search for the perfect Christmas tree. I kept a hefty part draft and part thoroughbred horse for just such a chore. After we chose a tree, the week before Christmas we pulled the tree down the mountain. The big horse pulled the tree with no effort although fresh snow piled up to his belly.

By the time March blustered its way past the peaks of the Rockies or blew toward the rolling hills from the Pacific, winter was eagerly wished away. Both man and beast in the Rockies anticipated spring while spring in California was awaited with trepidation. A California spring turned into a battle between winter and summer, with neither winning for the month of March and April. Oh, but spring in the Rockies, it was a promise of a new beginning. The down coats, the snowmobile boots and long underwear could be packed away in furthest corner of the closet.

Spring

Spring in California was blustery and mean. The last rains before the usual summer drought insisted on a last show. Blustery and damp winds that penetrated everything but Gortex chilled a cowboy to the bone as it wailed and whipped off the ocean. Spring always seemed caught in a fight between winter and summer with neither winning out until summer simply overpowered their squabble.

Calving time becomes spring's most important event in Southern California ranch country. Calving time arrives far earlier in the coastal mountains than in the Rockies. By the time March marched toward April, calves were already a month or two old, little tykes who attempted to outrun a swinging rope before branding and castrating determined their future. Branding season continued to be synonymous with spring and a social season for ranchers. Branding events were carefully planned by each ranch in the community to be sure everyone could show up on different weekends for the round up and branding. Those weekends were a fine time for our family. A time to visit, work at what we loved most, and a time to party. Each week we were invited to a different ranch. The big day usually started early, when the sun crept over the horizon we rounded up the cattle brought in from the back forties during the past week. The final roundup was a short journey because everyone was anxious to get started with the branding.

We fastened the cab-over camper to the pickup for our mobile baby sitter, and hitched the horse trailer to the truck. Of course, nothing short of a V-8 and a three quarter ton pickup would manage that kind of load. If there were any short-cuts to be made in our budget, it was never the pickup because of the man size jobs expected from this vehicle. We outfitted the camper with toys, coloring books, crayons and snacks. Because Shane was the oldest, our little baby sitter in a seven year old suit, he cared for his younger brother and entertained him while mom and dad were out pushing cattle into the home corral.

"Now you take good care of your brother, we'll be back in an hour." I reminded our little cowboy after riding up to the camper for one last check. But there were always plenty of folks around headquarters to look in on the kids and everyone expected to keep an eye out for all the little tykes running about. By the time the bawling and protesting herd was pushed into the corrals, the boys finished their morning snack and were ready to watch the show atop a corral post or explore barns and sheds. The men and women were busy in and around corrals that woke up with dust, bawling calves and mooing moms who were separated from their babies. The cowboys and cowgirls traded off sorting and cutting calves from their mammas, roping, branding, castrating, counting and recording a tally. The smell of singed hair from the glowing branding iron drifted over the corrals. After the last calf was branded, they were allowed back with their mammas to seek solace and a comforting lick from mom to soothe the hurt from the branding iron and the castrating knife. The reunion was bittersweet. The little tykes were soon separated from their mothers and shipped to market. If the spring crop had been good and the prices for cattle fair, the ranch might survive for another year. Spring was financial success or disaster. The rest of the year was primarily preparing for next spring.

Spring on a ranch in the Rockies is calving season but the season arrives later than in California. A calf born in February or March could hardly survive the brutal months at the end of winter. At Paradise Ranch, spring in the Rockies was also a time to bring the horses back from winter pasture.

In Parshall, the early spring sun thawed the frozen earth and during the night, turned the mushy blanket of snow over mud into cement.

Below Pikes Peak, where the Rampard Range towers over Paradise Ranch meadows, delicate columbines heralded spring with pale and dark purples, sky-blue and wisteria lavender. They concealed their delicate petals among tall meadow grass and gravitated toward the protection of aspen trees leafed out into a burst of creamy green. But just because the mountain world redecorated for spring didn't mean winter gave up its iron grip. Paradise Ranch nestled below Pikes Peak at an elevation of 8,600 feet at an altitude where spring and winter battle out their superiority throughout April and May. Sometimes a defiant winter would kick open the door for a surprise snowstorm in June.

When the Peak disappeared behind roiling clouds, mixing rain, wind and snow, it's a clue to the inevitable spring snow. Nature seems never satisfied to cover the thawing earth with an inch or two. No, she has to dump a foot of snow, sometimes two or three feet. The three-foot surprise was a great conversation topic. "Heck, couldn't even drive the pickup to the barn."

"Yea, been plowin' all day."

"Had to get the snow off the sheds, they would've collapsed."

"How are your horses out by Divide?"

"Couldn't check 'em. They'll survive a day, then we'll take feed to 'em."

During spring the melt down becomes a hurried affair, leaving corrals in knee deep mud, and horses caked with black, brown or gray mud for the next week. A currycomb is often insufficient to scrape off the dried layer of mud. Our boots were unrecognizable, unless you wore over boots. The Cowhand western store in town always counted on a brisk business selling overshoes in the spring when winter tenaciously clung to one final protest, howling, objecting and digging in like a stubborn mule.

During our year at the flyspecked feedlot, spring on the Colorado prairie was especially ill tempered. Near the Nebraska border, no gentleness represented spring. The wind blew more than any other time of year; corrals transform into a quagmire, and over boots were barely enough to keep the mud from squishing past the tops. At the feedlot, even the fattened steers in the corrals were discouraged and seemed to gaze past their corrals toward the greening pastures, thinking how stupid humans were to lock them up in a perpetual mud bath. Along with the steers, we had to make a concerted effort to appreciate the sprouting land and the endless furrows with tender green tips bursting through the black earth overnight that caused farmer's smiles and Joe grumbles. The return of winter's scourge destroyed our expectation of green grass, cottonwoods twinkling with new pale green growth, and ground we could walk without waders. The abrasive winter returned with blustering storms, racing across the unhindered land to form drifts so deep that roads and fences disappeared. The storms howled and whistled across unchallenging expanses, and they always busted onto the land when I hoped to escape the flatlands and its monotonous days for a reprieve in Denver.

Summer

The passing of spring on the flats of the Colorado Prairie meant that we might be abler to walk in dry corrals and soon we could butcher a fattened steer. Summer on the prairie announced its arrival with banging and rumbling from fear-inspiring lightening storms. Thunderclouds formed miles to the east or north, gathered in veracity and speed, roiling with contempt for anything attached to earth. Lightening struck with vengeance anything that stuck out of the earth, was wet, or made of metal. Nobody challenged lightening on the prairie. Tractors were abandoned, horses tied up in the barn, and we too fled to our house. The white frame farmhouses trembled with each blasting crack of thunder and the sky reeked of singed matter. After the storm, somebody often had a story to tell. "Did ya hear? Johnson's television set got blown up," or "I lost one of my cows. Got electrocuted 'cause the old bag pushed herself into a fence."

As summer thunderstorms growled their way across the flat defenseless land, we feared tornadoes with each storm. They rarely happened, but we noticed that folks felt special when they could talk about living in tornado country. Thunderstorms in themselves were plenty to contend with and provided decent entertainment, but tornado threats granted prairie folks a way to stand apart from the rest of the population.

Our feedlot summer was also the season for flies. As summer temperatures favored egg hatching, the fly population exploded with great gusto. They reveled in the piles of manure and congregated on every available screen on the old two-story farmhouse. Flycatchers had to be replaced every couple of days and fly swatters earned their keep. Summer also brought a bit of relief from stupefying boredom on the prairie. Nobody seemed to do anything in the winter. Farmers and their families hibernated, spring brought enough work to cut out any leisure activities for farm families, but by summer even stodgy old farmers were ready to detach from their tractors. Church bazaars, ethnic celebrations and parades were a pleasant diversion from watching fat steers get fatter on molasses and corn, or watching millions of flies on the screens.

In the Rockies, activities halted during spring and summer resumed at the beginning of summer. Summer was a relief from quiet times with not much happening. For the past snowed in and blustery months, boredom knocked on the cabin door and everyone felt a bit tired of wearing bulky down jackets. With spring's finicky days and unpredictability, summer was appreciated for its predictability. Warm days, cool nights, and soothing evenings. The blustering wind withdrew to other pastures, the biting cold with a wetness that seeped through jackets and warm pants gave up its fight. Pikes Peak shed its white coat and beckoned visitors to explore its lofty peak. The horses were not shedding their wooly coat all over a new sweater and muddy corrals dried within a few hours. Summer brought another round of exciting events, rodeos and horse shows, hundreds of rides into the backcountry, and new friendships as Paradise Ranch again opened for business. Summer brought moody weather, but bad mood weather usually changed within an hour or less. Soaked jeans and wet saddles dried in less than an hour under the potent high altitude sun.

Lightening storms marked nearly every afternoon at Paradise Ranch. The proximity to Pikes Peak was a perfect location for thunder and lightening. Every afternoon, as if planned on purpose, always after a ride had left the barn yard, a thunderstorm blew in with great fanfare, announcing itself by clapping and roaring and launched lightening randomly toward warm boulders and tall pines. When lightening hit a tree, it exploded with a resounding crack as it split down the middle. Dirty gray clouds galloped across the sky faster than a horse could outrun the ominous cells and both beast and man wisely found shelter. Waiting under a short tree not fodder for lightening, an impression on the mountain slope or a distance between warm human and equine bodies were necessary precautions. We avoided frightening the dudes and related the necessity of evading a lightening strike with a matter of fact attitude. "Come on folks, we might as well rest here for a while."

Many dudes were unfamiliar with lightening in the mountains and feared that their horses might bolt. "Won't my horse get scared?" The dude asked.

"Naw, they were born in this kinda weather." Most of the guests ended up drenched and the cowboys who brought slickers couldn't help but comment for the umpteenth time that they were smart enough to bring them and had warned everyone to roll up a slicker. "Better change those clothes, you sure got yourself wet," they hinted with a bit of a grin. Most guests didn't mind wet clothing because that was part of a western adventure. The horses also seemed to not mind getting wet because afterward they could contentedly roll in a mud hole and coat themselves against annoying flies.

No sooner had thunderstorms thrown the atmosphere into chaos, the rains passed and moved on to new destinations. Our ride emerged from our makeshift shelter and continued, a bit soggy, but relieved to again soak up the strength of the sun soothing the uncomfortable dampness. The sky and the earth and the trees and grass instantly burst into freshly laundered colors. The greens appeared deeper, the trees richer, an invisible paintbrush painted the sky brilliant azure, outlined by a few lingering clouds as white as bleached pillow cases. The earth smelled like freshly washed pine. Never a grumble seemed to cross a rider's lips, just the awe and the contentment that comes from being welcomed into nature's embrace.

Summer in Southern California was not soothing. It presented a mean, hot and dusty enemy that caused sweat and thirst. Temperatures climbed to ninety, than a hundred and as summer wore away, erased all vibrant colors and sparkling life of spring. Creeks dried up, and rivers diminished to a trickle. Animals were listless during the day and the rain an unknown phenomena in the forecast. The earth cracked open and left fissures that seemed to cry out for water. Everything turned yellow, brown, or golden; although the golden hills, like huge ocean waves, created their own unique splendor, but the harshness of the land could not soothe the eye.

Animals were easier to find at Rancho San Fernando Rey because they never wandered far from water tanks and congregated under century old oaks until the heat of the day gave way to the less blistering heat of the evening. Daytime heat sucked the strength out of beast and man; evening and night heat was a relief, although many an evening with a depressing ninety degrees lingered long after dark. Those nights were like sitting under a blanket that smothered all energy.

Summer days on a Southern California Ranch were carefully scheduled. Ride in the morning before sunrise, finish your roping or round up by mid morning. Work at something else during the mid-day heat or disappear for a siesta. Watering troughs for cattle were always a welcome relief for the cowboys. They dipped their hat into the cool water and then jammed the hat right back on their head, the liquid pouring over their dusty faces. A few good splashes on the clothes cooled body temperature, but within one hot breath, clothing dried. Sometimes cowboys were brave enough to take off their boots and jump in the tank while the horse spooked away from the commotion.

At Rancho San Fernando Rey, Joe and I found a watering tank that became our swimming pool away from home and our secret Shangri-La. The tank was large enough to water twenty or thirty cattle at once, hidden at an abandoned homestead. Wild blackberry bushes grew in profusion around the tank, and tracks of deer, bear and boar imprinted on the damp earth surrounding the tank. Oak trees shaded the run down homestead in a canyon hidden from civilization. This was our secret place to escape with the kids after another scorcher day. The coolness of the water was delicious, and the blackberries a special treat. Those were our blackberry evenings.

Summer in California also brought the danger of wild fires. Once a spark ignited the tinder dry brush, the fire galloped on a runaway path that could obliterate everything for miles and miles. Fires devoured valleys, stands of ancient oaks and whole mountains. Being vigilant for fires was an integral part of living on this thirsty and parched land in the summer. The wet winters that every rancher craved also sprouted waist high grass that dried into kindling and fuel to feed fires.

One particular July eve, after dark settled over the coastal range, we watched with awe and misgiving as the mountain ridge, dividing the coastal hills from the desert, glowed iridescent orange and red. The glow, faint at first as it ate its way up the east side of the mountain, grew in intensity until it topped the crest and continued to eat its way down the west side of the mountains. Rancho San Fernando Rey bordered the western side of the mountain and the fire threatened to race toward the ranch. By the second night, the fire swallowed the entire mountain and pale gray ash rained to earth as a warning of the hell that could follow. Nighttime winds felt stifling hot and we feared that the fire might descend toward the valley. Every rancher, cowboy and homeowner to the west of the mountain knew that this inferno could engulf their home and ranch. On the third night, the eerie blood orange glow continued to crawl toward civilization. The sky droned with airplanes dumping pink fire retardant and the whomp-whomp of choppers announced their mission to carry buckets of water from Lake Cachuma.

Those nights, ranch families slept fitfully, and tried to measure in miles how far the inferno was from home and worried with every gust of wind that the firefighters could not check twenty foot walls of racing flames erratically jumping this way or that depending on the winds. The whole scene turned into an eerie glimpse of hell.

Brave and determined fire fighters finally managed to bring the inferno under control. During the aftermath, the mountain stood like a monument to its devastation. Naked, black and lonely. Trees were gone, some hardy oaks a black and charred testament. The grass and impenetrable brush had disappeared and only ashes and black skeletons of brush remained of what was once shelter for pigs, snakes, deer and bear. The ranchers breathed their usual sigh of relief. "That was close."

One more threatening fire had been survived.

Summer in California brought those fears for every rancher. Each week without a fire turned out to be a time to breathe a sigh of relief with a worried glance toward the kindling dry brush and brittle grass. Ranchers relaxed a bit when ocean breezes brought fog to cool the land. Evenings became the time to live when the onshore air tempered the choking heat. That's when we barbecued, invited the neighbors for a lifesaving cool beer and opened the windows of the house to blow out the day's stale air. The swamp coolers ran non-stop during the worst of the summer. Sometimes we reminisced about pleasant summer days under the umbrella of clouds gathering over the Rocky Mountains, forgetting all about the blowing snow, the frozen pipes, and the frigid mornings when we had to feed the cattle in forty below.

9

The Revenge

Our nightmare began when Paradise Ranch closed its doors forever after the halcyon years of the dude ranch era. The nightmare of unemployment and trying to survive each day, each week and month without a paycheck and the worry over bills hovered like a vulture at our front door. So now what? Could Joe find cowboy work in the shadows of Pikes Peak?

"There ain't good jobs around here," Joe said, "we gotta move. I'll find me a good riding job in California. That's where they are."

Actually, the trouble started with a particular ad in the Western Livestock Journal after months of reading discouraging ads like: "Reliable man wanted to take over herd of Angus, fix fence, irrigate."

Joe cursed the ads." I'll be damned if I walk all day and fix fence. Read this one, they want a farmer, not a cowboy."

The ads continued to advertise for hired hands with farm experience to would work for poverty wages and live in a shack. Those were quickly crossed off. Some stated they wanted a single cowboy with no obligations. Cross those off. Joe's obligations included two little cowboys, two horses, two cats, two dogs and a wife. Some ads stated they raised purebred cattle or owned purebred horses and those were crossed off. Joe figured that people who raised purebred cattle probably treated them like pets and expected their ranch hand to wipe their rear ends.

Those people, as he called them, would have little need for a real cowboy. Cross all those ads off. Some jobs were offered on horse ranches. Cross them off also because Joe was suspicious about owners being city slickers and expecting the hired hand to cow tow to their spoiled horses.

"I know how those people are. They spoil their horses and then they want you to work with 'em without teaching 'em good manners."

Just when we had stretched hope as thin as a worn out rubber band, an ad promised the sun, the moon and stars to starving cowboys.

Million acre ranch seeking cowboy, Brangus operation, daily riding, prefer married man, own horses and dogs ok. Remodeled ranch home, new appliances, school bus to ranch. Can work into foreman position.

That ad started a nightmare we could not imagine. Joe already tasted the wild riding, roping and days spent on top of a horse. We wasted no time dropping a resume into the mailbox. Within two weeks, we headed to a new port in the storm of unemployment. We hoped we could get to California with enough money to buy groceries.

Our life savings depleted, we reassured ourselves this would be the job of jobs, and Joe would become foreman and retire at a grand ranch in the golden California hills. Our spirits soared along with the odometer as we rolled through New Mexico, Arizona, and into California.

Brimming with Tom Mix hat-size expectations, we arrived at the Hartford ranch during the blistering afternoon heat. As we turned off Interstate 5, our hearts sank a bit. The surrounding country looked as flat as the highway, divided by canals wide enough for small ships. Irrigation pipes perched on fields like giant praying mantis. The fields stretched in an unending sameness, disturbed by the occasional dust devil or a green John Deere. The monotonous farmland had not been part of our dream. Finally, hope replaced disappointment. In the distance, muted by the haze created from dust and irrigation, a tremendous coastal range rose like a gigantic beached walrus. Soon we distinguished details. Canyons carved hills like a slit cut into freshly rising dough, and waves upon waves of flaxen grass drifted toward the rising mountains. To our relief we headed toward those mountains at the end of a ruler straight dusty road, ranch buildings silhouetted against the golden hills, still far way and as tiny as toy houses spread out by a child.

When we finally rolled to a stop in front of our newly remodeled ranch house, the butterflies in our stomach returned. The house was plain, weathered, and square, perched like a shabby box in the shade of a massive oak. A small yard with dirt and no grass surrounded the house, encased by a feeble wooden fence that leaned like an old man on a cane. Porches enclosed the worn house on three sides; black dusty screens encased everything as if the wrapping should hide the house's disrepair. The entire house tilted to the west, and I was afraid if we stepped on the porch all at the same time, it would collapse from too many untended years and too much weariness. Inside the house, the wear and tear of too many uncaring occupants continued. The foreman who brought us here pointed out the brand new refrigerator and stove. He said the appliances were delivered just in time for our occupancy. He seemed proud of the two appliances, but I noticed that both appliances were the cheapest of cheap appliances. At least they work, I thought, providing we had enough money left to buy groceries.

I hid my disappointment but itched to express my displeasure as soon as the foreman left. Maybe the job itself was dynamite and we could fix the place up a bit if anything was worth fixing since the house looked like it might collapse under a new addition of paint or curtains. To cope with the growing distress, I conjured up images of moving to a new home as soon as they promoted Joe to that promised foreman job. I hated to admit that this house looked no better than the Mexican farm worker's shacks I had read about. The place reminded me of a home described in Grapes of Wrath. The foreman showed Joe the rest of the ranch while I walked around the house, feeling hopeless and trying to talk myself out of feeling that way. My kids explored, but soon joined me, not interested in the few square rooms that had as much personality as a shipping box. In the dining room I found the telephone and discovered the phone was an eight-party line. Perhaps an eight-party line could be a way to meet the neighbors?

Past the squeaky screen door in the kitchen, I watched as Joe and the foreman walked to a massive barn. Much less neglected than the house, handsomely weathered boards rose two stories to meet the hip roof. Corrals butting up against the side of the barn were home to our two horses. I spotted no other horses, no cows, or chickens. Our two dogs warily trailed Joe and the foreman, no doubt trying to figure out if there was any fun to be had like chasing cows or wild boars at this new and strange place.

Between the barn and the house, a tall gas tank perched on metal legs. The white paint had chipped off. I hoped we could gas up our pickup now and then. Next to the pump, short, stubby sheds with flat roofs kneeled in dried mud, and sagebrush covered the fencing surrounding the pens. As expected, the sheds and pens were in as much disrepair as my rickety home. I turned my attention back to the house and thought I might as well start unloading our cars. The moving van would arrive tomorrow, and although I wanted to send it back, pack the boys, the horses and dogs and turn right around to someplace less dreary, we didn't have a penny left to travel anywhere but the grocery store.

Joe started his job on Monday. He preferred to look forward to his new cowboy job and talked himself into higher expectations than my prediction. "One bad thing usually leads to another." I said after the kids were asleep.

"Well, bride, lets just wait and see. This is big country. Maybe the riding is really good."

I attempted to decorate our transient shack with curtains to brighten the dingy rooms. They helped cover up the bleakness, but nothing covered up the sagging floors and the flyspecked black screens. While I unpacked, measured and decorated, the day wore on with oppressing heat seeping through the thousand cracks and crevices in the old house. Joe did not come home at five. He did not come home at six. The boys and I ate in the kitchen, the windows flung open to catch an almost imperceptible evening breeze. Just before nightfall, Joe arrived. He looked hot, dirty, and tired, but we figured some days are just that way. Tomorrow might be a normal day. The long days persisted. Every day Joe returned home more dusty, hot and tired than the previous day, never until the last spark of light and just before the day sinks into the hand of night. I waited with dinner and a bad feeling in my stomach.

I enrolled Shane in kindergarten and the school bus picked him up each morning at the dusty gates to the ranch. Travis played in the house, and I planned to seed the yard to grow a patch of grass for the kids. Within a week I learned about the cheapest grocery stores and met my neighbors.

The neighbors also seemed disgruntled. They were an old wrinkled couple, his skinny legs bowed like an oblong 0 and his weathered face revealed too many years under the sun. They lived a mile down the dusty road, and the first thing I wanted discuss were the long hours and the shoddy houses, but they avoided the subject, most likely too frightened to lose their job if they discussed the atrocious conditions. They seemed resigned. As if life dishes out leftovers and you had better be grateful for a handout. A single cowboy might not mind complaining because he could move to someplace new. Sling his saddle over the sides of the pickup and drive to another place, maybe better, maybe worse.

Another ranch hand, a single drifting cowboy lived out in a line camp shack. He claimed to be happy to live way out with the coyotes and deer and didn't say much of anything. I guessed he would someday pick up his saddle and gear and move on to another outfit for a few months before he felt the urge to drift once more. Several young couples worked on the ranch, but they lived in town near the ranch's dairy. We were a bit jealous because their houses did not threaten to collapse and their children played in a green yard with bushes and flowers. The cowboy crew continued to endure the same twelve-hour days, the same riding in the hills incinerated by the sun without a noon break. Nobody complained because the other cowboys and their families were just as strapped for money and time to look for greener pastures. I put up with the sweltering heat spiked with humidity from thousands of irrigated acres of farmland. I rode my horse, but the foreman was disinterested in having a female along on their outings into the back forty. Even Coach and Black Puppy were not enthused with the beginning of each morning. Dogs learned how to judge a good from a bad ranch. They kept their distance or ignored the foreman, judging him as a man not suitable for their company.

The first weeks passed with traces of hope, but the traces disappeared as one month rolled over into the next. The foreman still had his heels dug in firmly with no intention to leave his position. The foreman's house was a pretty place on the outskirts of Gustine, with lots of bedrooms, an orchard, green grass, barns and corrals. He raised a dozen quarter horses and was absent whenever he pleased to work with his own horses.

I watched the first sprigs of grass poke through our own barren yard and felt jealous when thinking of the foreman's pretty home. Joe brought up the promise of a foreman position.

"Ain't no foreman job here," he explained.

"But," Joe insisted, "the ad said that this job could work into a foreman position."

Disinterested, the foreman shrugged. "Well, you never know, a foreman job on another Hartford ranch might come up someday. I didn't write the ad. The boss secretary probably didn't know what to write."

The faint glimmer of hope dimmed even more with each passing month. Hartford owned most of Crow's Landing, Gustine, the surrounding farms, canals, feed stores, tack shops, silos, and a million acres here and there, but no foreman job appeared on their horizon. The foreman continued to deny that the ranch advertised a cowboy job with an opportunity to advance. "You're lucky to find this job," the foreman announced with his usual rudeness. Like the other employees, we were afraid to speak our mind because we were poor and broke and couldn't afford to be without a job.

Fall drifted into winter. The grass I planted for the kids in our tiny front yard sprouted into a sparse carpet. Joe and the other ranch hands worked six days a week from sunup to sundown, and often after sundown. The house finally cooled and the humpback Diablo Range heaved a sigh of relief as the first rains soothed its blistered skin. On Sunday we tried to make the best of our disappointed life and hunted boar, four wheeled the boundless cattle range spreading to the hazy horizons of the Diablo Range and hauled our horses to local roping and barrel racing events.

During the six workdays, Joe complained a lot, but he dare not complain to anyone except his wife. For the time, we were helpless, and could only hope to save enough to move someplace else. At least, during the shortened winter days, Joe's twelve to fourteen-hour day changed to an eleven or ten hour day.

My dirty and tired husband finally confronted the foreman. "We got to get home earlier, I don't have time for anything. How about having shorter work days?"

The reference to the long hours instigated a barrage of insults and threats. "You can be replaced by a wetback, you ain't worth a nickel to me. I can fire you tomorrow. That goes for all of you."

The men grudgingly shut their mouth, and swallowing their pride; Joe barely containing his wrath. "God, I'd like to punch his lights out. Arrogant &#@*#" Joe dreamed about getting even, but we could do nothing because we were poor and stuck.

The cowboys and their families at the Hartford Ranch were not the only ones who found their rights trampled and ignored. The whole farm world seemed mis-used, mistreated and rebelling. We commiserated with the Mexican farm workers who were rising up to their human rights and objected to the unfairness they had shouldered for a hundred years. Caesar Chavez shouted throughout the land as he defended the defenseless. He shouted the word union, which gave courage to the workers and infuriated landowners. The battle captured the world's attention and it captured our attention. We witnessed the farm worker's battles, the insults, threats, cruel working conditions, poverty wages, and broken promises. Giants in the vineyard business fought to hold on to their superiority, as did other rich farmers. They built compounds with fences and barbwire to lock up the workers and lock out the union men. Shooting and killing broke out. The lettuce and other farm hands joined the grape pickers in their rage against this injustice. The wealthy San Joaquin valley transformed into a battleground between the haves and the have-nots. Caesar Chavez's rebellious retaliation was heard in every field, every feed store, along the endless dusty roads connecting one farm town to another. His voice was heard in every living room including our living room. The National Labor Relations Board had become the busiest government office in the country as scores of farm workers were fired for so much as looking at a union man. The Board fought in court to protect workers against the constitutional right to join a union.

We lived on the fringes of the battle, beyond the fields that were the sole and heart of the battle. The ranch seemed isolated from Chavez's mission. When I drove to town, armed guards patrolled farm fields, and compounds surrounded by a chain link fence waited, empty during the day, to harbor farm workers after a long, dusty, thirsty and backbreaking day. The valley seemed to return to the days of slavery and servitude. Property owners used excuses to lock up their work-ers. Picketing threatened to end in bloodshed. The farm owner's excuse to fight seemed little else but to hold on to cheap labor through abhorrent conditions. The farm workers were no worse off than we were on the ranch. At first, I could not see a connection between a grape or lettuce picker and a cowboy.

Soon I imagined ranch workers joining Caesar Chavez, although such a feat had never been attempted. Cowboys are an independent bunch, not the kind to assemble at any union meeting. Joe continued to come home in the darkness of night, discouraged and angry. Too tired to say much of anything, he ate his supper and fell asleep. His anger and his hopelessness fueled my energy. I was surprised the idea had not appeared when I first listened to Chavez's rebellious speeches and when I noticed the compounds and the guards patrolling fields.

The seed of revenge sprouted that evening. The union could represent the cowboys at the ranch. Why not? Hartford employed enough disgruntled ranch hands to organize into a union. I expected the opportunity might be welcome by angry families and single cowboys. Such an attempt, I knew, would be a historical event.

I mulled over the idea for the next week, allowing a brand new seed of hope to germinate. That week also brought a new discovery. Although I had been suspicious for a month, my rebellious nature did not kick in until the idea of a union for cowboys. Through new glasses, I checked on other troubling incidents. Soon after settling in, I had been given the job of picking up supplies at the ranch's own feed and tack store in Crow's Landing. The foreman supplied me with a shopping list that included supplies for ranch horses used in the cattle operation. After I purchased bridles, brushes, grain and the likes, the foreman collected most of the items I deposited in the barn. They were never seen again, nor used or fed to any ranch horse. I suspected the items were transferred to the foreman's residence and used for his personal horses. The week of my union idea, I started to copy receipts and kept track of the purchases for the ranch. I contrived a plan and although Joe agreed it was a good plan, he arrived every night with no energy left over to contribute to my grand scheme.

Before winter slipped into spring, I called Caesar Chavez's Farm Worker's Union. Within a week, two union leaders in suits and ties appeared at the ranch. Their interest perked. We met in secrecy because the union men said that the foreman wouldn't like the idea. Their statement sounded like the understatement of the year. We were asked to continue the secrecy until we could set up a vote. The union men also warned us that it was illegal to fire anyone because of union activities as long as they were not on company time. We started to recruit ranch hands and met at our house during the dark hours of late evening. The cowboys at first were suspicious and apprehensive. They didn't see themselves as part of the lettuce and grape pickers, but they all admitted wages were bad, working hours were worse, and the boss was bad news. They were also scared. Nobody had money to move or jobs to move to if they were fired. The cowboys liked the idea of decent wages and hours.

We met repeatedly in our kitchen. The meetings and contact with the union men had been difficult because of the party line. Telephone calls were never private when snoopy neighbors listened on the eight party line. Finally, voting time seemed a reality. Until the foreman fired Joe.

It happened over our party line telephone. The foreman called and simply stated in one sentence "Joe, you're fired." No reason, no preliminaries, no warning. The call arrived Sunday morning, the blackest Sunday of our already bleak existence. The foreman maliciously added, "You better be out in two days." Our hope and world collapsed. We figured someone snitched on our union activities. When Joe asked the reason for being fired, the foreman said that he didn't know how to ride, handle a horse or cattle.

After two days, the foreman arrived at our lopsided front step and yelled a lot of nonsense about throwing us out. "Be gone tonight," he shouted as he left in a hurry because he wasn't stupid enough to hang around a cowboy during that kind of confrontation. He was lucky that Joe figured he needed to cool his heels or the foreman would have a real reason to fire Joe. While packing and fretting and worrying, I called the union. They wanted to set up a vote immediately, but by now the cowboys and their families were thoroughly scared. Nobody could afford being fired. Nobody wanted to be as destitute as that family from Colorado.

The union men voiced their disappointment, but they were used to scared people who gave up their dreams. They referred us to the National Labor Relations Board to help us with legal matters. The Labor Relations Board sent out a man to talk about the matter. Another man in a suit and tie appeared at the ranch, but this time we were not concerned if the boss noticed the man in the city get up. We agreed to the Board's recommendation that we sue Hartford* ranch. After a deposition, they promised to take the case to court. A weak glowing ember of hope kept us forging ahead to pick up the pieces of our shattered life.

God must have been walking through the San Joaquin Valley during that trying time. He must have taken special notice of one particular cowboy' family with nowhere to go. He must have arranged for a job opening away from the battleground of northern California to the tranquility of a peaceful valley in the south. He chose a place that soothed a weary and discouraged cowboy. He chose Happy Canyon Ranch, perhaps to make up for so many miserable human beings that he hadn't intended to create, and the unhappy times on this disagreeable piece of earth.

The foreman stayed out of our way, but we figured he was probably watching us from afar, anxiously waiting for our departure. We wondered if Hartford executives ordered to fire Joe or if this had been the foreman's own agenda. If he had his own agenda, he had reason to worry. Revenge is sweet.

I was on a path of revenge not only with the Hartford ranch but the foreman's personal shenanigans. Before we hauled our horses and family south, I decided to attend to unfinished business. I had never seen or met the owner of Hartford ranch, but perhaps he was concerned over the unrest in his valley? Perhaps he might be interested in the foreman's activities? I sent him copies of receipts for horse supplies that were never used at the ranch. I wrote the owner a nice letter with an explanation that should have sunk the foreman as deep as the battleship Bismarck. As expected, I received no response, but I enjoyed the feeling of personal revenge while we waited for the National Labor Relations Board to take Hartford to court. A letter arrived before we left the San Joaquin valley. It stated we were not needed in court and could move to a new job. "We'll be in touch soon," we were reassured.

"At least somebody heard us," I said to Joe when the letter arrived.

"I just want to get the hell out of here," he answered.

I felt a thousand pounds of farm dirt fall off my shoulders as we left the dusty yard of the Hartford ranch in the rear view mirror.

Though hope returned, nagging uneasiness squatted as my passenger on the front seat when I drove the pickup and horse trailer to our new southern destination. Where would our quest for security end? Would it ever end? How could I find faith that we would find a place to camp for the rest of our lives? What if this vagabond life never ended? The green pastures that dry up, the bosses with no respect for a good man, the houses that were never our own, the money that was never enough, the change of schools and friends for the children?. I wanted that feeling to fly away. I wanted more than hope. I wanted to not need hope. I wanted to raise my children in one school, and I wanted to keep the same friends, and I wanted to look forward to someday going to my children's graduation and watch Joe retire in our own home. Instead, I rolled to another destination of unknowns.

I never asked Joe how he felt. Was he not concerned over drifting through life? I was afraid to ask him for I knew the answer. He would tell me what he told me at the beginning of our adventure as cowboy husband and wife. "This job will be the one, this time I'll be the foreman, and we'll save for a place of our own." As had I watched the sunburned wrinkles around his eyes increase and the hairline receding, the passage of time stared back. Where were we after all that time? Where were the dreams? Where was our own place in the sun? I knew the answer.

There was no money for our own place because we spent it on moving vans and treks back and forth over desert and mountains to a greener pasture and than back and forth over the same desert and mountains to a different pasture. No, I need not ask, I reminded the woman who had once been a carefree girl dreaming of becoming a cowgirl and cowboy's wife. I had achieved that dream, but at a price.

The trip south turned into a soul-searching journey. As the San Joaquin Valley reflected in the rear view mirror, I felt grateful to see the flat land and lonely farmhouses disappear in the distance. Coalinga crept into sight, the last dreary outpost before climbing through the desolate mountain range dividing the coastline from the checkered farmland. I drove from one world into the next world. I dared not hope that this world would be our last home. A place where I could raise the little cowboys and a place I could call my own. As I drove from the mountains, the coastal land welcomed me with soothing green pastures, Spanish villas, strips of riotous orange poppies lining the highway as if to light the way to Nirvana. My hopes soared despite my misgivings and long imprinted disappointments with my life as a cowboy's wife. With each mile, the charm of Southern California grew with spectacular splendor.

From Salinas our journey continued past green fields stretching to the river, lush in contrast to the unclothed coastal hills. Past Paso Robles, the land spilled toward the ocean and into the fertile Santa Maria valley. Beyond Santa Maria the orderly grids of farm fields changed back to cattle country, interrupted by a vineyard here and there.

Toward Santa Ynez, horse ranches changed to fabulous estates and as we neared Happy Canyon ranch, my hopes soared further. A neat, white-framed farmhouse peeked through cascading honeysuckle and climbing rose bushes, shaded by gigantic oaks and an apricot tree. Past the ranch home, a hip roofed barn the color of burnished red looked like a good home for our horses. White fences packaged the rest of the ranch. We were home. I avoided guessing for how long.

On an afternoon with a flawless blue sky above the maize colored hills, I tended my tomatoes when I heard the noise. I had heard it before. It was the red plane, as red as my Big Boy tomatoes, way up in the sky above the hills toward Lake Cachuma. I shaded my eyes to watch the red plane roar straight up. Silence followed before it plummeted earthward and disappeared beyond a hill. Then it roared into sight again. I wondered what kind of crazy person flew that red biplane. I also wondered what it was like to feel such freedom.

Six months after our move from hell to heaven, a plain envelope with National Labor Relations Board on the return address arrived in our mailbox. We had won the case. We were not compensated with large sums of money, but I could taste the sweetness of revenge. The foreman had been fired. The court ordered the owner of the Hartford ranch to post a public notice at conspicuous places on his ranch, apologizing for the treatment of his employees and for the unfair firing of a cowboy. He had also been ordered to call an assembly of ranch hands and apologize in person.

We never talked about the days in the San Joaquin Valley. Joe would have been suspect and mistrusted by every rancher in the Santa Ynez Valley for instigating union activities. We rejoiced that a nobody cowboy and his wife got the attention of a giant corporation for one brief moment in cowboy history. We figured the would remained brief and sink into oblivion. What's a cowboy's wife to do but continue down the same path of roses and locoweed?

*Hartford Ranch is a fictitious name

Epilogue

I hoped we would live at Happy Canyon Ranch for a hundred years but I knew those were dreams. The many pleasant sunny days were marred by darker thoughts I brought with me on the drive from San Joaquin Valley to our Happy Canyon home. The flight from the Hartford ranch cast shadows into my life as a cowboy's wife. But Joe remained a dreamer.

I recalled his words from a long time ago, when we sat on the porch of our fly-specked house in Sedgewick. He had known he should get some sleep because he had to get up early to gather a bunch of feeder steers for a prospective buyer, but instead he had reached across the dusky spaces with tired eyes, and allowed the vastness and stillness to surround him. The wind on that rare evening, instead of howling like a banshee, had brushed the prairie with a kiss. I thought I could hear the feeder steers munching their hay with nary a suspicion of what tomorrow would bring. Joe hadn't noticed that Black Pup had snuggled next to his leg until he felt the Airedale's cold nose push under his hand. He ruffled the faithful dog's rough fur. "I should 'of lived a hundred years ago."

I hadn't known if he talked to me or the dog. Black Pup wagged his stubby tail.

"I'd pack my saddlebags, swing up on my horse and ride off to Mexico, across the border. Where nobody knows me. Leave this damned, complicated life. I been born too late."

Neither I or the Black Pup had answered.

"You know, my granddaddy never owned his own spread, but by god, he was a proud man, and a cowboy back then was a man of a respectable reputation, no matter if he didn't own much more than a saddle. My folks never owned much either. They bought a good piece of land by the river up in Washington State, where daddy eked out a living when I was a little tyke. There wasn't money for fancy cars or fancy horses. Dad owned a couple of nags that were pretty good cow horses, but I remembered as a kid that those horses worked hard and Daddy didn't allow me to ride them just for the hell of it."

Black Pup had relished his master's soft voice on the porch, moving closer to him to lay his head on his master's lap.

"I can still picture myself running across the hills when I was just a tyke, imitating Daddy who rode proud with a few other cowboys, swinging their ropes and carrying the secrets of the Wild West on the backs of their horses."

Joe had scratched Black Pup's ears. "Damn, I wanted to be on the back of one of those horses, but my daddy said he wanted his son educated. Educated." Joe spoke into the night stalking rapidly over the prairie. "Son, my daddy lectured me in front of mamma, this is a hard life, you ain't gonna live your daddy's life. No woman today would be your wife. Look at your ma. Women today don't put up with what your poor ma puts up with. You're gonna go to college." Joe had paused, taking his hand away from Black Pup's head to drink from the can of lukewarm beer.

"All I wanted was to ride and I thought I was lucky 'cause there wasn't money for college after I graduated from High School. When I was eight, I already had to do a lot of the hard work, feed and clean the corrals, milk the cow when I really wanted to be on the back of a good horse. When I hit my twelfth birthday, daddy finally gave me my own horse. But he didn't give me a good horse. He gave me the meanest and ornery horse and I thought maybe Daddy didn't like me. I know now he wanted me to be a real cowboy. When I was twelve that summer, I become a cowboy in Daddy's eyes. That happened right after Brownie almost drowned me. Daddy sent me to swim the river on our ranch to gather a bunch of renegade cows on the island. The river had swollen from spring runoff, the shores muddy and slippery. Brownie refused to cross, slipped on the mud, fell on his side, thrashing on the shore of the river and finally he plunged into the river after my foot caught in a stirrup. I went under again and again. Finally, I managed to grab the horn with both hands when Brownie righted himself. Daddy said nothing when he saw me wet and caked with mud. I brought those renegades back to the ranch. I also said nothing, but I give my Daddy one look with a clear message. I'm a man now. Don't mess with me. Did you get them all? Daddy asked and I answered, did you think I couldn't?

At fourteen, I grew into a big and muscular boy and had to wear hand me down men's clothes. I earned money by shoeing the neighbor's horses so I could take out girls. The college my mamma and daddy dreamed about didn't happen. Couldn't afford college. That's when my Daddy wanted me to take over the ranch when I got done with the Army, but I couldn't live my dreams on the little homestead.

So I packed my duffel bag, my old saddle, stashed the anvil with shoeing equipment in the trunk of an old Chevy I bought from horseshoein' money and threw a bedroll and a few blankets on the front seat. One of the big outfits that still operated as if they lived in the 1800's hired me as a bronc buster. Part of the year I followed rodeos as a saddle bronc rider until I ran outa' money and then I hired on at a new ranch. At the rodeos, there were sure a lot of pretty girls that paid attention to me. But then," Joe's eyes returned from searching the empty spaces on the prairie, to the porch, "I got me one right here."

Black Pup had wagged his tail as if he agreed.

On a glorious morning, when the blustery March winds grudgingly gave in to the gentle warmth of spring, my horse neighed as I walked into the corral at Happy Canyon Ranch. The day started to arrive with a halo of gold crowning the horizon. Perhaps I was as much of a dreamer. Did I not live the dreams of my youth this very morning? None of us talked as we rode into the hills. The silence of the dawn discouraged talking. Steam from the horse's nostrils escaped into the cool morning air. The grass, a shag carpet of fertile greens and in places high enough to reach the horse's belly, shed teardrops against the rider's boots. In the stillness, the saddle leather creaked, the only sound aside from the horse's hoofs on the soft earth and an occasional snort from a disgruntled horse.

So far, we had located not one single cow or calf. Ragged patches of fog still clung near the river bottom and crept over grassy knolls, hiding the mammas and their babies. As we climbed higher, the heavy fog transformed into a curtain of gauze and at the very crest of the hill, we emerged into a dawn washed sapphire blue.

"God, it's beautiful," Joe said, reining in his bay horse and turning around in the saddle to look at me.

978-0-595-35933-2
0-595-35933-7

LaVergne, TN USA
08 March 2010
175248LV00001B/49/A